Meeting the Challenge

Using Love and Logic® to Help Children
Develop Attention and Behavior Skills

Meeting the Challenge

Using Love and Logic® to Help Children
Develop Attention and Behavior Skills

Jim Fay

Foster W. Cline, M.D.

Bob Sornson

 Love and Logic®

2207 Jackson Street
Golden, Colorado 80401-2300
www.loveandlogic.com
800-338-4065

The Love and Logic Institute, Inc.
2207 Jackson Street, Golden, CO 80401-2300
www.loveandlogic.com

First edition
First printing, 2000

Library of Congress Catalog Card Number: 00-102723
ISBN 1-930429-02-9

Project Coordinator: Carol Thomas
Editing by Linda Carlson, Eric, CO
Cover design by Michael Snell, Shade of the Cottonwood, Topeka, KS
Interior design by Michael Snell, Shade of the Cottonwood, Topeka, KS

Published and printed in the United States of America

Contents

Introduction

For more than two decades, we've been sharing the skills of parenting with Love and Logic. Effective parenting is based on love that is not permissive, love that doesn't tolerate disrespect, and love that is powerful enough to permit children to live with the consequences of their poor choices. When we treat them with empathy and respect, we can help our children focus their energy on making positive choices, learning to persist, and learning to believe in themselves.

Many parents have used the skills of Love and Logic to make their homes calmer, happier, more respectful places. We celebrate their parenting.

There are many wonderful books and tapes on parenting today, and ironically, there has never been a greater need. Many parents lack networks of support, wise eyes to guide them and encourage them at those times when parenting gets hard.

Schools see more troubled kids today than in years past, especially children with attentional difficulties and challenging behaviors. They are great kids, but they are challenging.

This book is dedicated to the belief that kids that are challenging can grow up to be wonderful adults. Some of these children have been diagnosed with attention deficit hyperactivity disorder (ADHD) or have been categorized in a variety of other ways. Others are called spoiled. This

book is about creating hope for all children with these problems...
regardless of their label. It's for parents who want a clearly explained
program to help their children become responsible, caring, persistent,
and confident. It's for educators who want to help in that process and
who are willing to work with families.

Many people have contributed to this effort. For more than twenty
years, Dr. Foster Cline has been my partner and friend. His intellect
and compassion are the fabric of Love and Logic. Shirley Fay has been
my partner even longer, wise and loving, she gives motivation and
strength. The Cline-Fay and School Consultant Services staffs keep
everything moving forward.

In recent years, Charles Fay has joined our staff and has contributed in
many ways to the thinking represented in this book. Dr. Ray Levy helped
us see how Love and Logic could be successfully used with children who
had difficulty sustaining attention.

Several years ago, Bob Sornson convinced me that parents and teachers
would want to learn more about using Love and Logic to help kids with
attention and related behavioral issues. Subsequently we offered our
first training in Livonia, Michigan. Then Bob convinced me that we
needed to capture and refine our ideas in this book. His belief in this
project gave it life. His understanding of the unique needs of each child
gives it depth.

This book is organized into five main sections. Chapters 1–4 describe
the fundamentals of great parenting. Using stories and explanations,
these chapters will help you learn to apply the simple rules of Love and
Logic in your life.

Chapters 5–9 focus on the special needs of children who struggle to
sustain attention. These children are not all the same, and each child
needs to be understood for his/her unique needs. Reading these chapters
will give you a better understanding of the unique needs of all children.

Chapters 10 and 11 are the heart of the book and describe a step-by-step
program for parents to use at home and for educators to use at school.

Chapters 12 and 13 describe situations where parents and educators work together to effectively help challenging children become responsible problem solvers.

The final chapters, 14–16, sum it all up and provide you with a clear plan for applying the rules of Love and Logic yourself.

We offer you this book with the hope that it will help you raise joyful, productive, and responsible children.

Jim Fay

chapter one

There is Hope!

"**Just** buy him an alarm clock," her friends told her. "He's old enough to get himself up. Quit babying him."

So she did. She talked with him for twenty minutes about how he was old enough. Together they set the clock. "Don't forget, you're responsible for getting yourself up," she reminded him as she turned off the light.

"O K , Mom, I'll try," Alex responded.

But it was not to be. In the morning, the alarm rang and rang. Finally she woke him up. Five minutes later, he was sound asleep again.

"Please hurry," she begged. "I can't be late for work again. Your bus has gone, and I'll drive you, but please hurry."

As usual, it was hard for Alex to get going. He couldn't find his favorite shirt. Then it was his backpack. He spilled his cereal. She felt it building up within her. She was on her knees, cleaning the mess. Her beautiful fourth grade boy had wandered into the family room and had turned on the TV. He was watching the weather forecast while her nylons were covered with milk and fruit loops, and once again she was going to be late for work.

The kitchen towel that was dripping milk and cereal trembled in her hand. Deep within her something screamed; **there has to be a better way!**

·····

One of the most frustrating things many parents have to deal with is a child who takes forever getting ready in the morning. Kids with attentional challenges or challenging behaviors may offer an extra dilemma. Parents may wonder, is my child capable of handling this task, or do I need to give extra reminders and special allowances?

Keep in mind that this story is more than merely about wake-up time. It's about persistence and following through. It's about the fact that challenging kids can learn to be responsible and think for themselves.

• • • • •

When she arrived at work late and checked her email, there was a reminder notice. PARENTING WORKSHOP DURING LUNCH. USING THE SKILLS OF LOVE AND LOGIC. ENJOY SOME LAUGHS.

I could use some laughs, she reflected.

Her friend, Edith in accounting, called her later in the morning. "Are you going?" she asked.

"I'm so busy. I probably shouldn't take the time. I've been late twice this week, and my work is piling up."

"Would you take a suggestion from a friend?" Edith asked gently.

"Of course I would, from you."

"Go to the workshop. I'll come too," Edith offered.

The workshop turned out to be fun. Stories and laughs were shared. And then the speaker told a story about a little boy who was out of control at home—or maybe he was *in* control of the home. Alex's mom couldn't believe it. The speaker was talking to her. Even though he was on the other side of the room, smiling at other people, this story was for her.

She started thinking and wrote a few notes. Avoid ranting, raving, and lectures, she wrote. Let consequences come unexpected—like a bolt of lightning—but do it with empathy and love. That way the bad decision becomes the bad guy and the parents can be the good guys.

• • • • •

It was a couple of weeks before she was ready to attempt it, but when she was, she sat down with Alex at bedtime. "Guess what, Alex," she said. "Tomorrow I'll be leaving for work on time. Isn't that great?"

Looking mildly curious, he fluffed his pillow until it looked comfy and waited for more.

"We're going to try the alarm clock again."

"Didn't work last time," he reminded her. "I just can't hear it. You know my ears have ADD."

For a moment she faltered. Maybe they do, she thought to herself. Then she shook off her doubt and ignored an incredibly strong urge to lecture him about the importance of getting to school and work on time, about personal responsibility and how much she loved him, and about how she didn't want him to turn out like Uncle Ralph.

"Goodnight sweetheart," was all she said.

In the morning, she heard the alarm ringing. After a few minutes, Alex must have shut it off, but there was no sound of his feet hitting the floor.

After dressing and getting a bit of breakfast for herself, she realized it was time to go. She found herself humming. Like a bolt of lightning, she thought as she entered Alex's room.

He raised his sleepy head. "Mom, I'm sorry. Will you drive me?"

"Oh, sweetheart, I'm leaving for work now," she said. "But don't worry. I've called the school and told them you missed the bus. Good-bye, sweetie."

"You're not leaving me home alone, are you? You can't do that. I'll call Social Services!" he hollered.

Somehow it made her feel better when he said that. "Don't worry," she responded. "I thought you might oversleep, so I made arrangements. Why don't you come into the kitchen and meet Mabel." With that she left for work.

It was a confused little boy who wandered into the kitchen that day. Little did he know how his life was about to change. Mabel was a big woman who had already enjoyed the privilege of raising five children of her own. She regarded Alex with a baleful stare. "Isn't this a school day?" she asked him.

"I missed the bus," Alex scowled back. "I want some Cocoa Puffs."

Mabel's reaction was disarming. She smiled broadly, then the smile turned into a shaking laugh. It took her a moment to catch her breath. "Here's the deal," explained Mabel in a loving tone. "You can get yourself a bowl of cereal. Then you're back in your room. Since this is a school day, I don't expect to be bothered by you during school hours. I don't want to see you, and I don't want to hear you. I'll let you know when it's time for lunch." Mabel never stopped smiling as she talked.

No day had ever seemed longer to Alex. The Gameboy in his room was gone. There was nothing to do but read. How could his mother do this to him? Around 4:30, he finally heard her come home. Opening his bedroom door, Alex saw his mother smiling, standing inside the door finishing a Dairy Queen hot fudge sundae and talking to Mabel.

He gave his mom his 'how could you do this to me?' look, but she didn't even seem to notice. "Alex, hi, sweetie!" she called. Then she came over to him and gave him a big hug.

"I had a terrible day," he protested.

"Oh, I know," she said sincerely.

"And I don't like her," he pointed at Mabel. "I was in my room all day."

"That must've been sad," said his mom. "But there's one thing more. Before Mabel goes home, you have to pay her."

Unable to find any words, Alex just looked at his mom. Finally words came to him. "But, I don't have any money."

"No problem," said Mabel. "Sometimes I get paid in toys. This Gameboy I found looks good. Is it yours?"

He nodded.

"Good. That'll do. Good-bye. Hope to see you again." As she went through the door, Mabel gave Alex's mom a little wink.

She put an arm around her beautiful boy. "I had a great day at work," she said to Alex. "Shall we take a nice walk before dinner?" No ranting, raving, guilt, or lectures she reminded herself.

· · · · ·

A few days later, she and Alex were having breakfast. It was almost time for the bus. "I'd better get going," he said to her.

"Thanks, Alex. I appreciate what a good job you're doing hearing your alarm."

He thought for a moment before responding. "It's funny. I think my ears are getting a whole lot smarter."

Love and Logic is a gentle, powerful way to
get kids to think and be responsible.

Love and Logic lets kids learn from their experiences
without seeing their parents as being mean.

chapter two

The Rules of Love and Logic

Love and Logic is designed to be used by real people in their homes and schools, so there can't be incredibly long lists of procedures and rules. If there were, I'd probably forget some of them.

The rules of Love and Logic for children with attention problems are the same as those for all other children, but some kids will just test you more. Some kids need more experience with intense consequences than others. Some kids need parents who have developed better skills at allowing consequences without anger, threats, lectures, and warnings.

When little Susie starts playing too loudly, all it takes is a quizzical look from her mom or dad for her to settle down and moderate her volume.

It almost seems unfair. When Tyrel gets going, he fails to notice "the look." When his mom gives a little coughing noise, he doesn't notice. Nor does he slow his activity when she stands up, poses menacingly, walks toward him, stands next to him, and finally puts her hand on his shoulder.

It takes a little more to get Tyrel's attention, but he's still able to learn. He may need more consistent consequences and more intense consequences—always delivered with love and empathy. Tyrel's parents may need more energy, help, support, and encouragement than other parents. Some kids are easier to discipline than others.

Over time, Tyrel's parents may notice that his personality and intelligence, combined with his energy and intense spirit, will allow Tyrel to become an incredibly wonderful and successful human being. Love and Logic can be a big help in his development!

Rule #1

Adults take care of themselves by providing limits in a loving way.

1. Adults avoid anger, threats, warnings, or lectures.
2. Adults use enforceable statements.
3. Children are offered choices within limits.
4. Limits are maintained with compassion, understanding, or empathy.

When Nancy, a mother from Michigan, is on the phone, sometimes her little ones get too noisy or try to attract her attention.

"Hey you guys," she whispers. "Would you like to play quietly in here or go play in your rooms?" Is Nancy a master of taking good care of herself?

Sometimes this approach might work. If it doesn't, then Nancy might have to make the choice for her children.

"Uh-oh. Uh-oh," she sings. By singing the words she avoids putting any anger into her face or tone of voice. "Bad decision. I guess it's time for you to go into your rooms to play."

"But we want to play near you," they entreat.

"I know. You can try again in a little while."

"But when can we come down?"

"Don't worry, sweetie. I'll let you know as soon as it's time."

"Not fair," says her five-year-old as she moves toward the bedroom.

I know, Nancy silently sings to herself. It helps her restrain the impulse to rant, rave, or lecture.

Rule #2

Childhood misbehavior is treated as an opportunity for gaining wisdom.

1. In a loving way, the adult holds the child accountable for solving his/her problems in a way that does not make a problem for others.
2. Children are offered choices within limits.

3. Adults use enforceable statements instead of threats and demands.
4. Adults provide delayed/extended consequences.
5. The adult's empathy is "locked in" before consequences are delivered.

When Zeke came home from vacation, he was so excited to see his bike, a cool, silver BMX. He kept looking at it as the family unloaded the car. When his friend David came riding over, Zeke jumped on the bike and started down the driveway. How sad!

Zeke's big sister started to run after him. "Your helmet!" she shouted. But he was already down the road and didn't hear. He was usually so good about remembering his helmet, but they'd been away from home for two weeks. Anyone could forget.

"Oh, Dad, he just forgot," his sister implored.

"I know."

A few minutes later, Zeke and David came peddling up the driveway. Zeke was smiling, enjoying the feeling of the breeze on his face.

His dad waved at him, then pointed to his head.

Suddenly, Zeke's eyes got big. He came slowly to his dad. "I forgot," he said.

"I know."

"I won't forget again."

"Good."

"What are you gonna do?"

"I don't know, sweetie," said his dad. "But David is here now. Let's talk about it later. Try not to worry about it."

> **The knowledge that a consequence is coming is a consequence in itself. All consequences are more effective when delivered with sincere empathy.**

A bit later in the day, Zeke found his bike hanging from the ceiling of the garage. "Dad, how long until I get it back?" he asked.

"I don't know," said his dad, putting his arm around Zeke's shoulder.

"Probably not until I quit worrying that you might forget to wear your helmet again and injure that beautiful brain of yours." Zeke's dad loves his son so much, it's hard to see him sad.

"When are you going to quit worrying?"

"I don't know, Zeke."

"I was really looking forward to riding my bike."

"I know, buddy."

Empathy drives the lesson home without making kids feel we're not on their side.

A few days later, Zeke's dad quit worrying about helmets, unannounced, and the bike came down. In some ways, he still worried about his beautiful son, because he knew that Zeke was more impulsive than some kids. He was glad he hadn't spoiled the learning by lecturing. Maybe I'm finally learning to keep my own mouth shut, he thought, so that Zeke can do the thinking.

A child's self-concept is strengthened by the ability to make three statements:
- **I am loved by the important people in my life.**
- **I have the skills I need to make it.**
- **I am capable of making good things happen in my life.**

Out of love for their children and fear that they might make mistakes, many parents make it hard for kids to learn. How? They either rescue them constantly, or they boss them around and never allow them to practice making decisions.

Some are helicopter parents. They hover over and rescue their children whenever trouble arises. They run lunches and permission slips to school; they solve problems with other children; they do homework and chores when their kids are tired or not feeling motivated. They feel uncomfortable imposing consequences. When they see their children hurting, they hurt too, so they bail them out.

Other parents are like drill sergeants. In an effort to instill discipline, they bark orders. They tell their kids what to do and when to do it. These parents are into power. Unfortunately, their kids get the message that they are not capable of making decisions. They become dependent on their parents and often resentful as well.

A dad from Kansas called me up and told me the following story. His twelve-year-old son had been arrested. "The police called and told me to come pick him up," he reported. "All the way down to the station I reminded myself, I've got to take care of myself and allow the problem to be my kid's problem. I don't need to holler, threaten, and then solve the problem for him. When I got down to the station, my son was so remorseful."

• • • • •

"Don't be mad," he said. "I don't know why I did it. It was the stupidest thing I've ever done. Promise me you won't be mad. I'll never do it again.

I'd been practicing my words on the way down to the police station. How can I be angry?" I asked him sincerely. "I love you and I feel so sad for all you're going to have to go through. I hope you're strong enough."

"What do you mean?" he asked.

"You're going to go to court." I said. "You're going to need a lawyer."

"You'll get me a lawyer, won't you?"

"Son," I told him. "Let me make you a promise. As long as you live, you'll never have to hire a lawyer for your father. And I never intend to hire one for you."

**Who's doing the thinking now? When you allow mistakes
to become learning experiences, kids gain the wisdom they
need for life in today's challenging world.**

"Oh, come on. I've gotta have a lawyer!" he implored. "You've gotta get me a lawyer. Billy's dad has already hired one for him."

Fighting back the temptation to launch into a lecture, I replied, "I know."

"I've gotta have a lawyer. What am I gonna do?"

"I don't know."

When we got home, my son stomped upstairs and went into his room. After a while, I saw him come down and get the Yellow Pages. Later he came to talk to me. "Dad. Lawyers are a rip-off. Six-hundred dollars is the cheapest I could get one."

"You got a lawyer who would represent you for $600? Now there's a bargain," I said. I kept my actual thoughts to myself.

"But I don't have $600," my son added. "What am I supposed to do?"

The response I'd been practicing worked again. "I don't know." Then I remembered the next part of helping kids to learn to be problem solvers. "Would you like to hear some ideas?" I asked.

He nodded.

"Did you know that in Kansas, dads can represent their own kids in juvenile court? Of course, I'm not trained, so I couldn't charge you $600. But I'd do it for half."

"You'd charge me?" he asked incredulously.

"Sure, for my time and effort. But only if you want me."

"I guess I'll take you," said my son. "Cause I don't have $600."

"Do you have $300?"

"No. But you know I'm good for it."

**Most mistakes can be wonderful learning opportunities...
if parents don't rant, rave, and rescue.**

"I've been taking this class," I told him. "They showed me how most mistakes can be turned into great learning opportunities. I'll tell you what. I'd be glad to advance you the $300 and at the same time teach you how a person can loan money to another person and be assured of getting their money back."

He just stared at me.

"Let's take a trip to the office supply store. They sell forms down there. I'll show you which ones to pick out."

We went to the store and picked out a promissory note. Back at home, he was filling it out at the table and started to get an attitude. "I don't get this."

"What?"

"Security for the loan."

"Oh, that's important," I replied. "That's where you list all the personal property you want me to repossess if you don't pay me back by this date here, September 1. If you don't pay me back, then I can take the property to the pawnshop and sell it, so I can get my money back. That way I'm not angry, and you're off the hook."

"Hey," he said defensively. "I shouldn't have to give you my stuff if I have trouble paying back my loan. All the kids have trouble paying off their loans."

"Thanks for telling me. I guess I'd rather not be your lawyer."

"Fine dad you are!" he snorted.

"Would you like a dad who gives away family money to people without getting it back?"

When he stomped away, I thought I was off his list of potential lawyers, but before long, he was back. He put the paper on the table in front of me. "I hope you're satisfied. None of my friends have to put up with this kind of stuff."

"I don't know if I'm satisfied," I said, looking at the note. "Will that stuff bring $300 down at the pawnshop?"

"Well, sure."

"I think I'd trust the owner of the pawnshop better," I said.

So the two of us took a trip to the pawnshop, and my son had the privilege of seeing collateral up close.

Consequences without anger will hold his feet to the fire.

The big day came, and we went to court. My boy stood up in front of a very imposing judge. "Do you have legal representation?" asked the judge.

"I think I do. My dad is doing it. He's not a real lawyer, but he's only charging me half." Then my son told the judge about our arrangement concerning the promissory note and the collateral.

"Young man, how do you plead?"

I stood up to be his lawyer. "Your Honor, my client wishes to plead guilty. But he's a good boy. He's a fine young man who made a mistake, and both he and his father know that's how young boys become good men. He's willing to live with the consequences. Today, he stands before the court to offer restitution, and he asks for a twelve-month deferred judgment."

I went on. "Your Honor, we realize that a six-month deferred judgment is possible in a case like this, but my son wants to show the court he can keep his nose clean for twelve months."

"So ruled," stated the judge. "Step back young man and have that loan paid back by September 1. And, if you should ever happen to come back into my court, bring your toothbrush."

A very stunned twelve-year-old boy walked out of the courtroom. He didn't have one word to say. All the way home in the car he was quiet. We went into the house, and he hung up his jacket. It wasn't until then that he spoke. "Dad," he said quietly. "You know what? You were awesome."

My kid likes me better now than before. I used to be afraid to hold him accountable. But now I know that if I do it with empathy and love, he doesn't get mad at me. Instead he gets to think about his own behavior or choices.

My boy spent much of the summer cleaning gutters and cutting lawns. He got to meet all of the old people in our neighborhood while he was looking for work. He got strong. He paid back his money, and he has money left over. I can't wait for him to make another great mistake.

Rule #1:

Adults take care of themselves by providing limits in a loving way.

Rule #2:

Childhood misbehavior is treated as an opportunity for gaining wisdom.

Summary

Some kids are tougher to discipline than others, that's for sure!
With the two simple rules of Love and Logic, parents can tame
even the toughest.

chapter three

Applying the Rules of Love and Logic

As we saw in the last chapter, the Love and Logic approach helps adults establish themselves as loving authority figures in the family, and it helps the child gain self-respect and problem-solving skills and raises the odds that your children will go on to become happy, successful adults.

Some children are downright easy to raise. They want to please, have a generally easygoing disposition, and notice a raised eyebrow or the slightest change in your voice and quickly adjust their behavior. Other children take more effort. They may be strong-willed, spirited children. Tyrel is a good example. Some children have incredible energy. Some have difficulty staying focused on the things adults find important. Some have had a bad start and may have difficulty believing that the adults should be the authority figures in the family.

These children will probably take some extra effort. More consistency, more significant learning experiences, and sometimes more intense consequences are needed. Of course, to be effective, all this must be given while maintaining a positive, loving relationship. The great thing about challenging kids is that they can become very successful, exciting, and responsible adults.

One of the great things about Love and Logic is that parents are always finding new ways to apply it to their lives. As we travel around the country, parents tell us wonderful stories that demonstrate the use of Love and Logic skills. In this chapter, you'll get to share a few of the ideas we've heard from parents who have begun to apply Love and Logic in their lives.

Neutralizing Arguments

Charles Fay heard the following story about a sixteen-year-old girl in Utah.

"I was so upset," her mother recalled. "She told me she was going to her girlfriend's house, and I happened to call and check. I don't know why. Probably just mother's intuition. When she wasn't there, I called her boyfriend's house. She was there and his parents were not."

• • • • •

"What are you going to do?" she demanded.

"I don't know," I told her. "I'm too upset to think clearly now. We'll talk when you get home. Try not to worry about it."

When she got home, she started in on me. "I am sixteen," she said.

"I know."

"I shouldn't have to check in with you."

"Some people think that way."

"I was so embarrassed."

"I know." I was practicing my Love and Logic "going brain-dead," so I wouldn't get drawn into an argument that would only go badly.

"What are you going to do?"

"I don't really know yet. Maybe after a good night's sleep I'll be able to think more clearly."

"You're not taking my car. I need my car to get to work. You can't take my car."

I chose not to argue about what I could or couldn't do. Then I called my friend that had introduced me to Love and Logic. She and her husband had lived through a similar experience.

The next morning my daughter came downstairs. It was Saturday, and she was dressed for work.

"Shall we have that talk now?" I asked her.

"Can't now, Mom. I have to get to work. Later." She rushed out the door, and I rushed to the window. I watched her eyes as she settled behind the wheel, started the car, and only then began to realize that something new was locked across the steering wheel—the Club!

That was the day I started treating myself with more respect. My daughter was mad, but that was also the day she started looking at me with more respect. We talk more now and argue less. It's calmer in our home.

Anger and frustration prove to kids that their parents can't handle them.

Some kids are so good at getting parents to argue and explain. If they are successful, they also learn that the "best" way to get what you want in life is through verbal manipulation. They can suck every ounce of energy from a trying-to-be-rational parent. Love and Logic parents try not to get sucked into this game of brain drain.

"Dad. I found this really cool yo-yo I want to buy. Can I have my allowance today?"

"You want a yo-yo?"

"Yes. Can I have my money?"

"Buddy, what day is allowance day?"

"Saturday. But, Dad, it's only two days early. Come on. David's dad gave him the money."

"Sounds like you really want it. But what day do I give allowance?"

"Dad, don't jerk me around. Come on."

"Sorry. And what day do I give allowance?"

"I really want to buy it."

"I know."

"You're being a jerk. Ever since you went to that class you just smile and say things like 'I know.'"

Holding back another "I know," this dad answered, "Probably so. And what day do I give out allowance?"

Doesn't it warm the heart to see a kid realize that his old tools for manipulation no longer work? Isn't it great when parents remember that ranting, raving, lecturing, and then finally giving in to manipulation are not good for their children? Kids are learning because parents are learning. Remember, the first step toward success with challenging kids is getting good at neutralizing the arguing by going brain-dead.

Setting Limits

Love and Logic parents are not permissive. We set firm limits but try to avoid using angry fighting words that lead to resentment and control battles.

We are slow to lecture and try to avoid telling our kids what they have just learned from a problem they created.

One little boy was having trouble eating enough good food at mealtime. He had always successfully used his big eyes and trembling lips to get tasty snacks between meals. Lectures on the need for good nutrition didn't work. Begging him to eat more healthy food at meals didn't work. Anger and threatening didn't work either. The little boy just cried, then Mom cried, then she got out the ice cream to make him happy.

Until she tried a new approach.

"Try to eat enough good food at lunch today, sweetie. We're cutting out snacks for awhile. Try to eat enough to get you to your next meal."

The four-year-old boy was unimpressed. He'd heard it all before. In twenty minutes the dishes were cleared. There were no lectures. His mom didn't beg him to finish his sandwich or his soup.

Half an hour after lunch, he began his usual routine.

"I'm hungry." His big eyes looked sad.

"I know," said Mom.

"I need some food."

"I know."

"I'm really hungry," he persisted.

"Don't worry, sweetheart. I'll be serving a wonderful dinner when Dad gets home."

Now most four-year-olds who have successfully manipulated for food won't give up easily. "Bring me candy," he escalated the manipulation.

"Uh-oh," she sang sweetly. "Uh-oh. I don't like being yelled at with a mean voice. Feel free to stay with me if you can use a pleasant voice and nice words." (The better the parent sings these words, the more powerful they become.)

When parents don't act worried, kids click right into worrying.

Something was wrong. Mom wasn't lecturing. She wasn't pleading. She wasn't even getting mad or red in the face. And, she wasn't giving in.

"I want food," he stomped. "I need cookies."

"Uh-oh," she sang again. She had practiced using these gentle sounds so she wouldn't start ranting or lecturing. "Sounds like a little recovery time coming up." Instantly, she whisked him off to his room.

"When can I come out?" he pleaded, wondering who this alien woman was.

"Don't worry, sweetie. I'll let you know. Probably when you are sweet again. Have a nice little fit, if it helps."

**When Love and Logic parents talk to their kids, they use
thinking words instead of fighting words.**

At dinner that night, she used similar words.

"Hope you get enough food to get you to your next meal."

As he started to eat, a look of wonder came over his face. "Mom, when is our next meal after dinner?"

"I guess that would be breakfast," she replied.

"Breakfast in the morning?" he clarified. (Notice who is doing the thinking now.)

Fighting words invite disobedience by demanding that children "Do what I say" without treating them with respect.

When we use fighting words, we invite resistance:

"Get started on your homework right now!"
"Don't you look at me like that."
"You cannot go outside until you clean your room."

Nobody likes to be spoken to like that. By using thinking words and enforceable statements, we set limits without telling our kids what they have to do this minute:

"Feel free to go outside as soon as your homework is done."
"I'll be glad to listen to you as soon as your voice is as calm as mine."
"You can use my car as long as I don't worry about the use of alcohol or drugs."

Let's try a little practice session. Fill in the blanks:

Fighting Words	Thinking Words
Clean your hands right now!	I'll be serving dinner to kids with clean hands.
You are not going anywhere this weekend until all your chores are done.	Feel free . . .
You'll never drive my car again.	Feel free . . .
	I'll be giving out allowance on Saturday as usual.
Show me some respect. I mean it!	I'll be glad to . . .
You're not going out without your coat.	Feel free . . .
	Feel free to come back into the room as soon as you're feeling calm.

Your kids want limits, but most kids will test them to assure themselves that the limits are firm. They need to know we mean what we say. Try to deliver consequences with love and empathy. If we lecture and deliver consequences with anger, most kids will feel resentment toward us rather than thinking about their poor decisions.

If at the moment you cannot deliver the consequence with empathy, wait until you can.

Thinking words, empathy, neutralizing arguments, and giving choices when appropriate are the ingredients for successfully establishing limits with our kids.

Use of Choices

Love and Logic parents are always thinking. We want to be firm, loving authority figures, and yet we never want to take more control than we need. We want our children to make choices, sometimes to even make poor choices and experience the consequences so they'll get motivated to avoid costly mistakes.

When parents pull in the reins too tightly, kids resist and are filled with anger. When parents do not provide firm limits, kids are confused and insecure and begin making choices they are not prepared to handle.

A fifteen-year-old girl asked her parents to host a party for her friends, but with a special condition: NO PARENTAL SUPERVISION.

"Parents can't be around," she explained. "I'd be embarrassed. None of my friends would want to come. Surely you trust me? I can't have my parents around."

Her parents said they'd need some time to think about it. The next day they offered three choices:

1. We'll be at the party, but we'll try to be unobtrusive.
2. You can hire professional adult supervisors, and we'll go out to a movie.
3. You can have unsupervised parties when you have your own home.

Choices change the whole complexion of a control battle. They set reasonable options within limits, and they cause your child to think. Sometimes they offer the opportunity for your child to make mistakes and learn from the consequences. Choices let your child hear that you trust their ability to make a decision.

There are many choices that are easy to offer:

• Would you like to wear mittens or gloves?
• Would you like milk or juice?
• Would you like a bedtime story or a song?
• Would you like to set your alarm for 7:00 A.M. or 6:45 A.M.?
• Would you like to do the dishes now or before bed?

Some choices require the parent to be ready to make a choice if the child does not:

• Are you going to school with your clothes on your body or in a bag?
• Would you like to start homework after school or after dinner?
• My car will be leaving in five minutes. Will you be leaving the restaurant hungry or full?
• Would you rather pick up your toys or hire me to do it?
• Do you two want to settle your problem quietly or go outside and continue your argument?

Some choices should never be given (e.g., "Molly! Would you like to be round or flat?"). When three-year-old Molly starts to run into a busy street, it is not the time to give choices.

When it is appropriate, nonthreatening choices give children a chance to take some control over their own problems.

Rules for giving choices:

1. Select choices you can live with.
2. Be willing to let your child live with his/her decision.
3. Never offer choices when a child is in danger.
4. Never give choices unless you are willing to make a choice if the child does not.
5. Offer choices in a calm, nonthreatening manner.

   "Feel free to _____ or _____."

   "Would you rather _____ or _____ ?"
6. Offer choices before the child can say "no" to your request.

The 5-Step Problem-Solving Strategy

Love and Logic parents want kids to learn to solve their own problems. We want our kids to develop a little voice that lives in the back of their heads and says, "How's my next decision going to affect me?"

Sadly, out of love, many parents steal opportunities to learn away from their children:

"Mom, Katie was mean to me at school."

"She was? That makes me so mad. I don't know why you even like that girl. She's so selfish. Don't you worry, dear. I'm calling up her mother right now. Katie's just going to have to apologize, or else . . ."

**The best solution to any problem lies inside the skin
of the person who has the problem.**

"Mom, Katie was mean to me at school."

"She was? That's so sad. What are you going to do?"

"I don't know. Sometimes she's just so mean. She ignores me."

"And how does that make you feel?"

"Lousy."

"What are you going to do?"

"I don't know."

"Do you want me to share some ideas about what other kids might do in a situation like yours?"

"Yes."

"Some kids would quit talking to Katie forever. How would that work for you?"

"She's my best friend. I can't do that."

"Oh. Want another idea?"

"I suppose."

"Some kids would wait for a friendly moment, then tell her how they feel when being ignored. How might that work?"

"I'm not sure. It might be embarrassing."

"Want any more ideas?"

"No thanks. Not right now."

"Good luck, sweetie. Let me know how it works out."

"What are you going to do?" sends a power message:
You are capable of handling your problems.

The best solution to any problem lies inside the skin
of the person who has the problem.

Protecting our kids from the possibility of making a bad decision is a little like saying, "You're way too inadequate to solve this problem on your own. Fortunately, you have me, your wise and experienced parent to help you out once again."

The 5-Step Problem-Solving Strategy helps adults open the door to responsible problem solving by the person who owns the problem.

"Mom, David keeps pestering me and getting me in trouble on the bus."

"That's sad, Sam. You look pretty upset."

"I am upset."

"What are you going to do?" Mom asked.

"I don't know what to do. But the bus driver gave me a warning today."

"Bummer. Would you like to hear what other kids have tried in situations like yours?"

"I suppose."

"Well, some kids wouldn't sit near David. How would that work for you?"

"That's no good. He's my best friend."

"I know. Want another idea?"

Sam nods.

"Some kids would take a seat near the front of the bus so the driver can keep an eye on things. How would that work for you?"

"It might. But we like to sit near the back with the fourth graders."

"Want any more ideas?"

"Sure," said Sam.

"Some kids would talk to their friend and come up with their own plan. How does that sound to you?"

"Don't you have any better ideas?" asked Sam.

"I can't think of any. But good luck. Let me know how it works out."

Sam's mother avoided making the bus problem her own. She sent messages of empathy and confidence. Then she gave him permission to solve the problem in his own way. Did you notice the five steps?

Step One: Express empathy.
• "How sad."
• "I bet that feels bad."

Step Two: Send a power message.
• "What are you going to do?"

Step Three: Offer choices.
• "Would you like to hear what other kids have tried?"

Step Four: Have the child state the consequences or make a judgment.
• "And how will that work?"

Step Five: Give permission for your child to solve the problem or not solve the problem.
• "Good luck. I hope it works out."

Recently, a minister told me about his sixteen-year-old son. This minister was just beginning to learn about Love and Logic when he got a call from his son at 7:30 in the morning.

"Dad. I've got a flat tire. I'm over at school."

Pushing back his initial urge to jump in the other car and rush to solve this problem for his son, Reverend White paused. Empathy, he remembered. Lead with empathy.

"Bummer," he said to his son. "What are you going to do?"

"I don't know. I've never changed a tire. There's a big bolt sticking out of the tire."

"Want some ideas?"

"Yeah."

"Some guys find a friend who knows about changing tires. Would that work for you?"

"Probably. Dan knows about cars. But how do I get the tire fixed? That spare tire is tiny."

"Dan might have some ideas," said the minister. "Or you could take it to a gas station you trust, or to a tire store."

"What if they can't fix it? The hole looks big," said his son.

Reverend White remembered. "We bought those tires at Sam's Club last month. They might still be on warranty."

"But I've never returned a tire or had one fixed."

"I know, buddy. Right now I need to leave. Talk to you tonight. Good luck!"

It takes practice for parents to begin to enjoy watching their kids struggle to solve their problems. For many of us, there is a deep need to be needed, on top of the incredible love we hold for our children and the desire to keep them happy.

It was almost supper time when his son came in from his busy day. He somehow looked taller.

"Dad, the tire was wrecked," he explained. "After school, we changed the flat and drove to Asher's station, but they couldn't fix it. So I drove to Sam's Club, and they gave me a new one. You had the receipt right in the glove box. And then we went back to Asher's and they changed the tire. They even loaded the spare back into the trunk."

Reverend White watched his son. He reflected on how close he had come to not letting his boy grow stronger today.

"Dad," said his son. "Do you think I could invite Dan over to dinner tomorrow? He was a big help."

Empathy with Consequences

When George brought home his fifth grade report card, he had on his biggest, saddest eyes.

"Oh, George. Those teachers just don't understand you, do they?"

"I think Mrs. Watson hates me," whined George. "Mom, don't make me go back. School is ruining my self-concept."

Sadly, George has learned to elicit sympathy and avoid consequences. He's learned to avoid taking responsibility while neatly shifting the burden to someone else. If he continues in this pattern, he'll become a person who does not believe he can handle difficult problems and who fails to learn perseverance.

Using the principles of Love and Logic, George's parents would continue to show him love but would expect him to handle the problem:

"Oh, George. These grades are awful. You must feel bad."

"My teachers hate me."

"Really? How sad. What are you going to do?"

"Maybe we should home school."

"I guess that's an idea. I'd have to quit my job. We'd have to move to a smaller house. Do you think that's a realistic option?"

"No, probably not."

"Let me know if you need some ideas. But remember, George. I'll love you no matter how many years it takes you to get through fifth grade."

Our job is not to keep kids from making mistakes, but to help them learn from them.

At age five, Mary still sometimes fools around at the dinner table. Her dad has bought into consequences for poor behavior, but sometimes forgets about the empathy.

"That's it. You are done," he says with anger in his voice. "I'm tired of all that noise and rocking your chair. Get up to your room for the rest of the night!"

This of course causes tears and resentment, and dinner is not much fun for anybody.

Using Love and Logic Mary's dad would have taken care of himself while showing genuine love and respect for his daughter:

"Mary. I could use a really peaceful dinner tonight. Feel free to stay if there is no yelling or chair tipping."

One parent I know lets her kids finish their supper in the laundry room if they are causing the meal to be a lousy experience for the rest of the family. Another parent uses a few minutes of time on the "thinking rug" to give the family a break from rudeness. Enjoying family mealtimes helps to build the bonds of a lifetime. Good food, fun, laughter, and conversation bring kids home throughout their lives.

Anger and sarcasm create resentment and often cause a child to think about your anger rather than about his poor decisions.

It was cold in Colorado when nine-year-old Brian started out of the house without his mittens. Holding back her old impulses, Brian's mom said nothing. He was beginning to make so much progress. Since they had gotten timeout and food issues worked out at home, he was doing better at school. And he hardly ever forgot his chores anymore.

Now she watched as the snow fell in big flakes. Brian and his friend David were making a fort. In a couple of minutes Brian came bursting back into the house.

"Mom, my hands are freezing! Where are my mittens?"

She took his hands in her own, warming them.

"Where do you suppose?"

"In the mitten box!" He grabbed the mittens and raced outside.

Through the window, she watched him. It was hard learning to hold her tongue, to avoid the lectures and reminders that stole away his opportunities to learn by experiencing small natural consequences. He was starting to think ahead more on his own, as she reminded him less and less. She watched him playing. His hat fell off, and he kicked it out of his way into the snow. She raised her hand to knock on the window, then stopped.

Some kids need more experience with consequences to learn to think ahead. Ranting, raving, lectures, and reminders often steal these opportunities for learning.

Matt was rummaging through the garage. His dad could hear him going through the toolbox, then the ball barrel, then the woodpile. Then Matt went back upstairs to search again in his room. Finally there was the sound of dejected footsteps on the stairs, and Matt appeared.

"Dad, I've looked everywhere, and I can't find it."

Matt's dad knew without asking what his beautiful second grade boy was looking for. It was his most valued material possession, his Boy Scout knife.

Putting an arm around the boy, Matt's dad held him for a moment and considered his options. He could rant, rave, and lecture about the value of tools and the danger of leaving a knife unattended. Or he could give in to his impulse to help his boy and take away his sadness by purchasing a brand new knife. Instead, he decided to let his son experience consequences with empathy.

"That's so sad," he offered. "What are you going to do?"

"I don't know. I've looked everywhere."

"Want to hear some ideas about what other kids might try?" Dad asked.

Matt had heard this question before and nodded sadly.

"Some kids hire their sister to help them look in all the places a knife could hide. How would that work for you?"

"That's no good," said Matt. "She's no better at looking than me. Besides, I've already looked."

"Want another idea?"

Again Matt nodded.

"Some kids call up their grandmother. They use their whiniest voice and beg her to buy a new knife. Would that work?"

For a moment Matt's eyes brightened. Then he smiled. "That could work. I'll bet Grandma would offer to buy me a knife, but Mom would kill me, and you know it."

For a moment they both smiled and snuggled. Then Matt asked, "Any more great ideas?"

"Nope. I think that's it. I'm sorry you lost your knife. I know how much you liked it."

"Dad, I hate it when you're sad for me."

"Why?"

"Because that means it's my problem, and not yours."

For Love and Logic to work, the child must believe we are on his side.

There will be times when you are dealing with a problem and you can't seem to find an immediate natural or logical consequence. If no consequence comes to mind, it is often better to take your time and think of an appropriate response rather than acting in haste or anger. You can buy time by saying something like:

- "Uh-oh. Bad decision. I'm not sure what I'm going to do about this, but I'll get back to you. Try not to worry about it."
- "I've never been the parent of a teenager before. I'm not sure what to do right now. I'll be calling some of my friends, and then I'll let you know. Try not to worry in the meantime."
- "I'm not sure how to react to that. I'll think about it and talk to you in the morning. Try not to worry."

Delaying consequences gives us time to think, ask friends or advisors, or reread this book. And our kids have time to wonder about and agonize over the possible consequences.

Empathy drives the learning deep into their little hearts.

When "try not to worry about it" is used consistently, kids soon learn that "try" is the trigger word meaning "big problem for the kid."

Practicing empathy while allowing appropriate consequences is crucial to and at the heart of Love and Logic parenting. Empathy takes the place of anger or the urge to overprotect that may come to us at times and sends the unspoken message that you love your child and are on her side. Allowing appropriate consequences sends the message that your child is capable of making good decisions.

Many parents find that it helps to practice one specific empathetic response so that it becomes automatic and replaces the tendency to quickly overprotect or get angry.

Before getting angry or sucked into your child's problem, try using one of the following responses:

- "That's so sad."
- "Uh-oh. You do have a problem."
- "What a bummer!"

• "Oh. That's never good."
• "That's terrible. But I know you can figure out what to do."
• "That's sad. What are you going to do?"
• "Wow. I'm glad that's not my report card (grade, problem, etc.). You must be feeling bad. What can you do?"

Many parents have discovered that memorizing and using the same empathetic response helps empathy become automatic for them.

Allowing consequences while being empathetic is one of the toughest parts of Love and Logic parenting. You won't always get it right. Nobody does. Just keep practicing.

Love and Logic helps us send the messages we want to send to our children: We love you. We're on your side. You are capable of handling problems. Mistakes are part of life, just learn from them. Even when you make a mistake, we continue to love you.

chapter four

The Potential of Challenging Children

Her strong three-year-old voice called out, "I won't go!"

She wiggled angrily as her mother carried her to the thinking rug for the third time that day. "I don't want to," she insisted.

"I'll let you know when you can get off," her mother said calmly.

This was a practiced phrase. Her beautiful little Cindy, with the reddish hair and flashing eyes, had earned many visits to the thinking rug. Recovery time, they called it. It offered Cindy a few minutes to recover from a bad decision. And it offered her mother a few moments of peace of mind, not having to wonder where Cindy might be.

Cindy cried unhappily for a moment then quieted herself, and it was calm in the house. Her mother returned to the kitchen and shut the cupboard door, where a moment before she'd found her darling girl hanging by one hand from the third shelf, trying to reach the chocolate chip cookies.

The phone rang, and her thoughts were absorbed in the conversation. When she hung up the receiver, she noticed a small movement by the door. It was Cindy, watching quietly.

"It's been a long time, Mom. Can I get off now?" Cindy asked quietly.

Her mother realized then that she'd been on the phone almost twenty minutes. That was much longer than the three or four minutes of thinking time she usually required.

"Just one thing," said her mother. Cindy came close as her mom bent down to her level, and they shared a hug.

"Can I play outside with Bobby?"

"Sure, sweetie."

Cindy's brother Matt and his friend David were in the yard, and so was their new four-year-old neighbor, Bobby. Matt and David were trying to ignore him.

She watched as her strong-willed daughter ran out to play, and she smiled at the sight. Cindy was wearing purple pants, a yellow shirt, and a wildly colorful flower-print skirt that fluttered as she ran. It was an outfit of Cindy's own design. She had her own ideas.

Cindy's mom watched as her daughter grabbed Bobby by the hand and pulled him toward the sandbox. For a moment he resisted, acting like he would rather play with the big boys, but Cindy was persistent as usual.

There was a quality of persistence about Cindy that seemed so familiar. Cindy's mom thought then of her own mother, who had died a couple of years ago. She had shared that same quality of persistence. And God knows she needed it after her husband died when their kids were still young. Her name was Marie. That was Cindy's middle name. Marie raised six kids with a strength and dedication that only faith and an incredibly strong will could muster. There was no reverse on her gearshift. She would set a goal and then work until it was achieved. In all the years until her passing, her children never once heard her complain about how hard it was. She had those sparkling eyes, just like Cindy. In her last months, she would hold Cindy on her lap and look into her sparkling, clear baby eyes.

Out on the street, there was a squeal of tires and an angry shout. Cindy's mom quickly went to the front porch and watched Sarah's red Camaro weave down the road. Not again, she thought sadly.

Sarah was her sixteen-year-old neighbor. For years, she'd watched as Sarah grew older and the problems grew bigger. Sarah was a beautiful girl, but her eyes didn't have that sparkle. They were sad eyes.

When she was small, Sarah had never been made to stay in a recovery chair, room, or rug. Her parents had tried to persuade her to be sweet.

They often reminded and sometimes threatened, but she was a challenging kid. When she became upset, her parents held her and reassured her. She threw great tantrums, and they tried to calm her. Sarah made most of the food choices, and so there were snacks available at all times.

She had never really learned to delay gratification, or to calm herself, or to persist at difficult tasks in the early years. And then there was school. The demands of school seemed to make things worse.

Sarah was smart, but she got frustrated easily when kids wouldn't do as she demanded. She'd retaliate quickly against classmates, and sometimes teachers. They tried a couple of psychologists and an antidepressant medication. After her little brother was born, things got even worse. She didn't want to share. She'd write her name on certain boxes of cereal, waffles, and even soup cans. These were not to be shared with Jason.

And now Sarah was sixteen, with her own red car; a high intensity kid with a high intensity car. A strong will, poor adaptability, some distractibility, negative moods, and difficulty adjusting to change. It made Cindy's mom so sad.

She walked back to the kitchen and watched the kids in the yard. Matt and David were chasing Cindy and Bobby. The little ones squealed with delight as the big ones chased.

Cindy ducked under the picnic table and stated loudly, "This is safe. You can't get me here."

Matt tried to grab her leg, but she smacked his hand and grinned. "I'm safe," she reminded.

Maybe it was just a thought, but for a moment Cindy's mom felt the spirit of Harry Houdini in the yard, impulsive, persistent, and daring, helping this three-year-old girl.

Cindy was now stretched under the picnic table on her belly, examining an anthill. "These little ants are carrying sand from one spot to another!" Cindy shouted. And for a moment there might have been the spirit of Marie Curry, dedicated to learning, defying conventional norms, focused on the moment.

Then the game of chase was over, and Cindy ran to the trapeze that hung from the swingset. With her meaty little three-year-old hands, Cindy hung from the bar and pulled her feet a few inches up into the air. And for a moment there was the spirit of Wilma Rudolph, struggling to walk with braces on her legs, learning to run faster and faster.

Cindy's mom heard her husband pull into the garage and went to meet him. Then they came back to the kitchen window and watched together. Cindy and Bobby were in the sandbox. He wanted the maize and blue sand shovel, but Cindy was holding on tightly. For a moment they tussled in the sand, and in that moment the spirit of Martin Luther King Jr. was there, unrelenting, holding on to his sense of justice, standing up to a force of unquestionably greater physical strength.

Abandoning the hope of getting the blue shovel, Bobby took a bucket and dug holes on his side of the sandbox. Cindy's mom and dad wondered at the tenacity of their daughter. As they did, their hearts were touched by the spirits of many tenacious and challenging children who had become wondrous adults.

The spirit of Winston Churchill was there, holding fast against the forces of darkness. Thomas Edison was there, always thinking, seeing possibilities that no one else could see. Sojourner Truth was there, bringing families of slaves to freedom, taking unwise risks for a worthy cause. Benjamin Franklin was there, laughing, writing stories, running away from his apprenticeship, swimming, inventing principles of freedom, and flying a kite in the middle of an electrical storm. The spirits of many children who struggled and succeeded to manage their energy, enthusiasm, attention, thoughts, and dreams reached out to them in a whisper.

"She's wonderful, strong, and spirited. Help her know her strengths. Help her learn to use her spirit in the right ways. Guide her with love and with respect. Please don't make her smaller than she is by treating her with anger or resentment. Help her learn to use her energy wisely. You have the strength to raise this strong-willed child."

Maybe it was just a shared thought rather than a whisper. But in the years to come, it would be a moment they often remembered. In moments of challenge, it gave them comfort. Especially when they were tired. Especially when they might have considered trading Cindy for a compliant, low-energy, unimaginative child.

The moment shimmered, and then it was memory. Cindy's mom finished getting dinner ready, while Cindy's dad went upstairs to change his clothes. The backdoor slammed.

"Mom. You've got to come!" called Matt.

"What's wrong?" asked his mother.

"It's Cindy. She's throwing sand at everybody again. I told her, but she won't quit. And now Bobby's crying 'cause there's sand in his eyes."

"I'm coming," she replied. Then softly to herself she practiced, "Bad decision, Cindy. Looks like we need a little recovery time."

· · · · ·

Challenging children can become strong-willed problems or strong-willed problem solvers. The difference is whether they are held accountable for their own decisions and given an opportunity to learn and be motivated by their mistakes.

The rules of Love and Logic give parents a guide for helping their children develop responsible behavior.

In Chapters 5 through 9, you will be offered information and ideas that apply to children with attention problems. Even if your child doesn't have attention problems, you may wish to pick up a few of these ideas. You'll find they apply to all kids in one way or another.

chapter five

Variance

There is a danger that comes with the use of a label like attention deficit hyperactivity disorder. Describing someone as a person with A.D.H.D. implies a built-in condition over which she has no control. Some people may view her as defective, incapable of greatness. More importantly, the child herself may learn to accept lowered expectations and fail to cherish her blend of intelligence, personality, organization and processing style, sensory preferences, motivation, and other traits that make her unique.

Every child's attentional difficulties are unique, and every child's learning strengths are unique. By looking carefully at each challenging child we can remember to value their strengths while giving them the support they truly need.

James

Consider James. He was evaluated and given a diagnosis of attention deficit hyperactivity disorder, inattentive type, as a first grader. In second grade, he came to me for an evaluation. James's mother was concerned that he was doing poorly in school and particularly concerned that he had begun to dislike going to school. His mother had given Ritalin to James for a while during the previous school year, but discontinued its use because it seemed to affect his sleep. James had an excellent second grade teacher, who was also concerned about his unwillingness to try at school.

Using informal assessment techniques, I evaluated James to determine what he knew and what he could do. He explained to me that he didn't enjoy reading, but he liked having books read to him. I read to him for a few minutes, then asked him to read to me. Because he was such a nice kid, he readily complied.

He had good reasons for not enjoying reading. He read haltingly. Frequently, he had to stop to figure out words. Even if he read a word in one sentence, he needed to decode it again in the next sentence. Using his finger to help him keep track of his place, James still got lost. By the time he finished reading one sentence, he had likely forgotten much of the content because of the level of effort he was putting into decoding individual words.

Despite his frustration, James was a sweet kid. He tried to perform well. On tasks of auditory memory, he excelled. When asked to follow a moving pencil tip with his eyes as it came toward his face, he had difficulty. His eyes watered and looked away after a few seconds. He experienced similar difficulty tracking an object from left-to-right.

Holding a pencil three feet in front of him, I asked, "How many pencils do you see?"

He responded appropriately. When asked the same question at eighteen inches, there was no answer. Twelve inches, no answer.

Not yet sure what was happening, I asked him to do some printing. He leaned his head way to the left and close to the table and held the pencil tightly in his right hand. James had difficulty remembering how to spell words and often omitted capitalization and punctuation. His writing was nothing like his conversation.

Coming back to the pencil in front of the eyes, James softly admitted that when the pencil was near, he saw two. The same thing occurred at times when he was reading. He'd see double, or it would get blurry. His eyes would get tired and wet.

In a conversation later with James's mother, I learned that his sibling was a good reader, but his father was not. James's gross motor skills were excellent, but he had always avoided coloring, puzzles, cutting, and the like. He spent countless hours watching TV and videos and playing Nintendo.

James had real difficulty sustaining attention in some circumstances. That difficulty was particularly exacerbated when he was trying to work with his hands and eyes within his nearpoint visual field.

Helping James improve his attentional skills was not nearly enough. He also needed significant help to learn to use his eyes together within the nearpoint before he was going to be successful with a reasonable expenditure of effort.

Brent

Then there was Brent. His mother brought him to me as a high school sophomore. He was a good-looking and well-dressed young man.

Brent sat placidly while his mother expressed her concerns. He was not getting work done at school. He was not turning in assignments. There must be something wrong with his ability to do the work. There must be something making the work too hard for him.

He had been on medication for more than four years, his mother explained. But sometimes he forgot to take it unless she reminded him. When his mother left the room, Brent pleasantly began to work with me. His reading was normal. His conversation skills were excellent. He described his recent vacation to Hawaii. His auditory processes and memory were more than adequate, in spite of the fact that he was smoking dope daily. All his friends were doing the same, he explained. Brent's visual system and memory were good. His balance was good. His math skills were a little bit low. "I haven't done any math homework in a couple of years," he explained.

"What do you hope to be someday?" I asked.

Brent shrugged, "Maybe a pilot or an architect."

"Is it important to you?"

"No."

"What is?"

"Hanging out with my friends."

"Are they good friends?"

"Not really," he explained. "They don't really care about me. We just do things together. "

Brent told me he had no chores at home and that his dad was going to give him a car in June if he started to do better in school.

He was a nice boy with perfectly intact thinking skills and a loving, supportive family, but sadly, Brent's level of personal motivation was low. He was always given the things he wanted, protected when he screwed up, and had learned to give nothing back to his family or community.

Michael

Michael was a different case. At age fourteen, he already weighed almost two hundred pounds. He was quiet and gentle. Michael had been diagnosed as having an attention deficit and learning disability. I was his teacher in the first years of my career, and I didn't know much. I thought he was lazy and slow.

But something about Michael just didn't fit. He was always so nice. Even when I ragged on him, he'd smile and try harder, without much to show for his effort. He hardly talked. When he did, his words and sentences were often hard to understand.

Michael's parents were also kind people, who reassured me that he liked coming to school. I couldn't imagine how. In my second year with Michael, I began to look harder, working on spoken language as an aspect of the development of his written language. He garbled words. He tried hard, but couldn't restate simple four-word sentences. Even three-word sentences were reshaped in his memory. Finally, the limitations of his auditory memory became clear. Michael couldn't remember or restate sounds in a complex order. His ability to store and retrieve sounds in order was severely lacking.

In this case, my lack of experience turned out to be a benefit to

Michael. I didn't realize that a fifteen-year-old boy couldn't improve such basic memory and language skills. So we began to work, and Michael began to improve. He learned to say three-syllable words. He learned to hold words in his memory. He began to talk more. He no longer avoided answering questions. I no longer thought of him as lazy and stupid. Michael, I'm sorry it took me so long.

Alex

When Alex's mother came to see me, she had a prescription for Ritalin in her hand that she didn't want to use. The doctor had given it to her when Alex was being seen for an ear infection. He was six. His mother wanted to talk about alternatives.

Alex was certainly a busy little guy. He moved. He touched things. He didn't especially enjoy sitting still at a desk or table for a long while. Alex had been born slightly premature, but was released from the hospital after just one week. He was often colicky as a baby. His formula had to be changed. He experienced chronic ear infections as a toddler and eventually had tubes inserted.

Alex's mother thought that, compared with other children, Alex's motor skills were slow to develop. He still used training wheels on his bike. He couldn't catch a ball very well, and he couldn't begin to skip. Alex did not enjoy playing with puzzles. He occasionally played with blocks, but refused to spend time drawing or coloring. He preferred to watch TV or run around the yard.

I just love it when parents bring in a young child for whom so much can still be done to make learning develop easily and normally. Alex avoided table work for a variety of good reasons. His fine-motor and visual-motor skills were poorly developed. This had a lot to do with the fact that his large muscle control was still developing. He needed movement and gross-motor play before he could stabilize his body adequately for small muscle work. Adding to his difficulty, Alex's balance was still not very good, probably because of his chronic ear infections. Alex's lack of balance interfered with the use of his body for activities that require steadiness.

His mother described his eating habits. Alex craved sugar and ate cheese at least twice a day. He avoided many vegetables but ate starchy foods to excess. None of his doctors had ever mentioned the relationship between food cravings or nutrition to allergy and ear infection.

A sound nutritional program, activities to enhance balance and motor skills, a severe restriction on TV, video, and Nintendo, an emphasis on fine-motor activities to develop visual-motor and visual-memory skills, and a family dose of Love and Logic became part of Alex's life for the next eight months.

After eight months, his mother called for another appointment. When she came in, she told me life was much better, and then she began to cry. She told me she wasn't embarrassed by Alex anymore. She could take him to the mall. She even felt for the first time that she could take him to family gatherings without expecting him to embarrass them horribly with his behavior.

Every child with attentional difficulties is different.
Each one deserves a careful analysis of visual and auditory
processes and motor-skill and language-skill development. Each one
needs the opportunity to develop the thinking skills that are
related to attention, the movement skills that are related to agility
and physical success, and an awareness of how he or
she learns best as an individual.

chapter six

Diagnosing and Misdiagnosing Children with Attention Problems

Making a diagnosis of A.D.H.D. is fairly simple for many professionals (and of course, some parents make the diagnosis before the child ever sees a professional!) However, because so many different problems can contribute to these symptoms, just what the symptoms might *mean* and how to go about helping the child can be fairly complicated issues.

Many children show hyperactivity and inattention. A.D.H.D. is essentially a *behavioral* diagnosis. And although true A.D.H.D. runs in families, there is no blood or metabolic test that is specific to identify the problem. So familial A.D.H.D. is partly a diagnosis of exclusion. Did Mom or Dad have the problem when they were in school? Do they have continuing problems now? Do other immediate family members have the problem?

Anxiety in children can cause them to be hyperactive and inattentive and impulsive and hard to manage. So can a variety of other problems, including such common diagnoses as:

Childhood depression
Fetal alcohol syndrome
Fetal alcohol effect

Oppositional defiant disorder
Reactive attachment disorder of childhood
Various metabolic and neurological disorders

Although Ritalin and other stimulants help with true A.D.H.D. *symptoms*, it is essential for causal factors to be diagnosed accurately so that specific treatment can be implemented.

Jake R. was seen in therapy in Evergreen, Colorado, in 1994. He had been diagnosed elsewhere as having A.D.H.D., however, he had other symptoms not characteristic of A.D.H.D.:

- He was cruel to animals; and unlike many children, he had no remorse for the cruelty he inflicted on the family pets. His mom noted that all family pets became endangered species around Jake.
- He had a hard time showing any affection to his parents.
- When he was a small child, he would walk off with strangers.
- His distraught mother noted, "It's as if our love makes no difference to Jake."
- And Jake did not like to be held. When his father was asked if Jake had ever been cuddly, he wryly replied, "Holding Jake was like holding one hundred elbows! When is that cuddly!?"
- Jake hoarded food. His room was filled with half-eaten pieces of food, which, after becoming moldy were hidden under the bed.

It was no wonder that Ritalin alone was no help to Jake. He had the typical symptoms of an attachment disordered child! And he needed specific therapy directed toward his inability to love and relate to others. After holding sessions, Jake was relaxed, quiet, and responsive. His Ritalin was discontinued, and he no longer appeared to need the medication.

Just as the symptoms of A.D.H.D. occur in many different illnesses, so A.D.H.D. has many different beginnings. I have been working with children and their families for thirty years, and two things are *very clear*.

- A higher percentage of children fragment and have thought or learning disorders than was the case in the past.
- Many children with the behavioral problems diagnosed as A.D.H.D. would *not* have been so diagnosed in the past.

So why are we having an epidemic of A.D.H.D. diagnoses? Why has this problem blossomed? Where does it come from?

It is fairly easy to pick out early manifestations of A.D.H.D. It is not unusual to see an American five- or six-year-old dump out the Legos and stare at them, clueless. Such children don't have the slightest idea what to do with Legos. The scene repeats itself all across America, with minor variations. For Christmas, a seven-year-old girl was given Lincoln Logs. She was mildly curious at first. She tried briefly to put them together and then quit, saying, "It's too hard." In an unfocused way, she wandered into the bedroom, turned on the TV, and watched a Disney video.

Out on the front line, our schools literally reel as across America hundreds of thousands, if not millions, of kids are diagnosed with attention deficit disorder. It is a diagnosis that has reached epidemic proportions. All across the land, parents seek answers to help them understand their learning disabled or attention disordered children.

What is this epidemic of attention deficit hyperactivity disorder? How is it defined? Briefly, A.D.H.D. children's thinking fragments easily. It is hard for them to focus and carry through on a task. Their attention wanders. Often the children are impulsive, and often they have behavior problems. It does not seem to be a problem born of poor parenting, because high-achieving, loving, and responsive parents have children who are part of the epidemic. There is good indication that some aspects of attention deficit hyperactivity disorder are genetic. As is the case with many learning disorders, the father or mother may have had similar problems when they were younger. But is genetics enough to account for this epidemic? No, because genetic disorders are never epidemic in nature. Purely genetic disorders tend to have stable numbers or, if severe, are self-limiting. No, something other than genetics must account for the epidemic.

First, in attempting to understand the possible causes of the problem, it is important to see how the definition of attention deficit hyperactivity disorder has changed over time. Twenty-five years ago, when I was a young psychiatrist in training at the University of Washington, attention deficit hyperactivity disorder was seen as a *true disorder of attention.* At that time, it was believed that children diagnosed with A.D.H.D. fragmented easily and that they could not pay attention to television shows. This is no longer true. Modern authority after modern authority stress that attention deficit hyperactivity disordered children can pay attention to TV and are able to play video games. As a matter of fact, far from not being able to attend to television, the playing of video games or watching TV is often used in the primary grades as a reinforcer or reward for behavioral disturbed and learning disturbed children. Videotapes are used as a teaching tool across the primary and elementary grade spectrum with increasing frequency.

Far from being *primarily* an attention problem, attention deficit hyperactivity disorder might now more correctly be labeled an *intention* disorder. Children fragment when they should be intending to do something—to accomplish a goal, start or complete a project. In my experience as a child psychiatrist it appears the majority of children labeled attention deficit hyperactivity disordered have no problem at all if they are being entertained, playing a video game, or watching TV. They can and do sustain attention! The entire problem seems to revolve around getting the job done, whether the job is putting Legos together, building with Lincoln Logs, focusing on a Monopoly game, or completing a school assignment.

In the last analysis, it may not be important whether or not the epidemic is really an attention problem or an intention problem. Regardless of possible professional disagreements over symptoms, almost all professional observers, in both the fields of education and child therapy, are in unanimous agreement that there is an epidemic problem that affects the learning ability of America's children. To understand the problem, it is essential to look at the neurological development of children. Particularly, it is important to look at neurological development during the early years.

The importance of the first year for both cognitive and personality development cannot be overemphasized. During the first year of life, it has been estimated that half of a lifetime's knowledge is gained. During the first year, the infant organizes visual perception, auditory reception, learns reciprocal response, develops loving and/or conflicted relationships, and lays the foundation for gross motor skills. What a year!

A newborn human infant might be seen as one of God's most helpless creatures. It has rudimentary rooting reflexes, it can track sound and, in some cases, sight. It exhibits a Moro embrace reflex (limb extension) if it is dropped. It is arguably able to recognize certain sounds it could have learned in utero. Finally, infants exhibit a Babinski reflex (toes extend when the bottom of the foot is stimulated). The Babinski reflex simply shows that there is a lack of neural insulation or myelinization between the foot and the brain. Basically it demonstrates areas of neural disconnection. Almost all creatures in the animal kingdom have better survival techniques, more knowledge of the world, and are neurologically "sharper" than a newborn human. It might be said that "to find something dumber than a newborn human, one might check out a squash, or cucumber, or rock." Certainly the average frog or ant has better-developed reflexes and a greater understanding of the world in which it exists.

However, the neurons are literally churning during the early years of brain development. It is estimated that at the moment of birth, the infant is producing 250,000 neurons a minute! During the early years there is an almost magical dance that takes place between the developing brain and environmental stimulation. This interaction results in a real human being. If the environment does not provide the right stimulation or infants and toddlers are neglected, studies have shown that the child, for all intents and purposes, grows up functionally retarded.

At each early stage of brain growth, there is neurological readiness for internalizing certain concepts based on development. Much of the societal breakdown that the United States is now experiencing is secondary to the importance of millions of infants and toddlers not being exposed to the appropriate environmental stimulation at the necessary developmental age.

Before looking at the developmental stages, it is essential to briefly explore the "critical period" theory. This theory of development holds that there is an optimal time for particular types of learning. It holds that if the environment does not give the essential stimulation at the critical period, the optimal time for learning that concept, or method of thinking, is irreversibly lost. The theory holds, for instance, that language development should best take place in the second and third years of life. This is not to say that some people cannot learn a completely foreign language at a later time (English to Chinese or Arabic, for instance), but that it is much more difficult for most of us to learn a language at a later time. Obviously, the longer the environment "deprives" the individual of the critical input, the more difficult it will be to learn the concept or skill later. In twenty-five years of doing therapy, I have found that some forms of deprivation during the first years of life may be impossible to overcome later, in spite of years of therapy.

First Year Development Briefly Explored

The importance of the early years of life, particularly the first three years, is directly related to the major thrust of this chapter. Generally, the earlier the year, the more important it is for later cognitive and personal development. The importance of the first year of life simply cannot be overemphasized. The first year lays the foundation for four essential and related human thought and personality traits:

- Causal thinking
- The foundation for conscience
- Basic trust
- The ability to delay gratification

The average American doesn't fully realize the essential role the first year plays in laying the foundation of these four essential variables. Upon these variables civilization is built. If we meet a person walking the streets at night who has not developed these personality traits, we're dead. Without them, civilization as we know it would be lost!

If children are abused, neglected, or moved from caretaker to caretaker or suffer from unrelieved or unrelievable pain, they show their anxiety though hyperactivity and difficulty in focusing. So almost all severely disturbed children who have first year of life problems also exhibit most of the signs of A.D.H.D.

Causal Thinking

It might be said that civilization is truly built on causal thinking, which is the ability to understand that one act may cause another. A baby learns that when he cries and fusses, his mother will come. He learns that by sucking a breast or bottle his hunger is satisfied. When causal thinking is lacking, no civilization can either develop or be maintained. Causal thinking is closely related to the ability to delay gratification and to plan action.

Conscience Development

Conscience development can only take place with the growth of causal thinking, the latter being a necessary prerequisite. The rudimentary foundation of conscience takes place in the first months of life when a child learns:

"My actions can make Mom happy. When she's happy, things turn out well for me." Empathy is the ability to put ourselves in another person's shoes and think of their feelings. This is a first step in the development of conscience. This can only occur if there is consistent early nurturing from a mothering figure. Abuse and neglect, which are accompanied by inconsistency and pain, destroy the development of both causal thinking and conscience. "Planful" thinking is only possible if the infant lives in a consistent environment, and conscience can only develop in the presence of loving responses. Only individuals with a conscience can feel remorse, have a poor self-image, feel honestly guilty, or want to mend their ways.

Basic Trust

Psychologist Eric Erickson, in his pivotal article "The Eight Stages of Man" (Erik H. Erikson, *Childhood and Society*—second edition (Norton) 247-274.), noted that the task of the first year of life is the development of "basic trust." This, too, can only develop in a consistent loving environment. Basic trust, upon which all functional human relationships must be based, is the knowledge that people are generally good and that we all, in one way or another, can get along.

Today in America there are more children being raised in abusive and unloving environments than ever before. Some will grow to be individuals who are classified as "psychopathic" or "sociopathic." These are people who don't care about others and who have little conscience and no basic trust. Such people kill others without remorse. Although they are incapable of engaging in genuine long-term loving relationships, they are able to have sex and produce their own children—children whom they are incapable of loving and parenting, who will, in turn, produce others like themselves in geometrically increasing numbers.

The Ability to Delay Gratification

Everyone knows that good things come only with time; that patience is a virtue; that haste makes waste. While there may be times when these homilies are not true, almost always, persistence, perseverance, and planning pay off. The foundation for the essential ability to delay gratification is laid down in the first year of life, when a mother says, "Wait a minute honey, I'm coming," or when the child quits crying as he watches his food being prepared, knowing he is about to be fed—at last! When a person has to have their gratification now, when waiting is impossible, then almost all higher-order thinking, from the ability to avoid HIV or build a bank account to the ability to hold a job or build a city, is lost. In America today there is a great hue and cry about the necessity to educate people about HIV. This may not be the best use of time, energy, and money! Every little kid already knows about the dangers of HIV. The problem is, there are a lot of folks out there who just can't wait to have sex (i.e., have not learned to delay gratification)!

Almost every paper, almost every news magazine, is filled with articles on how to stop the violence. A recent *Parade* article by Bill Moyers is typical. The suggestions were:

- Allow judges to have more discretion to supervise and incarcerate serious offenders.
- Make penalties for violent crime sure and predictable.
- Get young people involved in volunteer services.
- Establish mandatory training for neglectful parents.

All the solutions deal with violence itself, which is only a symptom of the deeper underlying problem—the fact that millions of Americans don't think clearly and don't care. They have poor causal thinking and lack a conscience. Now that's what I call a problem.

Second Year Development Briefly Explored

Happenings in the second year of life also impact the development of signs of A.D.H.D. The tasks of the child's second year of life are to learn discipline and learn to obey a loving external authority figure. Generally, we might say that the tasks of the second year of life are to learn "come, sit, go, no, stay" messages from a loving authority figure. It is only the child's ability to respond lovingly to the requests of others that eventually allows parents to encourage and permit autonomy and independence, which are the goals of the second year of life.

Disobedient toddlers who don't respond to their parents' requests live in an anxiety-filled world where they are "boss," where limits are uncertain, and where parental frustration mirrors the toddler's anxiety.

Weighted down by these emotions, the child is generally slow to learn, impulsive, and appears to be "hyperactive."

Thus, a "normal" first year, with its foundation of basic trust, and a "normal" second year, with its elements of control, limits, and rules that the child must internalize, are essential for the development of a child who can focus and learn normally.

The fact that they have had poor experiences in the first two years of life explains the difficulty in learning exhibited by a large number of American children. All preschool, kindergarten, and primary classrooms across the land are filled with learning-disturbed, impulsive children, some diagnosed as A.D.H.D., who come from broken families, families with one parent, absent parents, and/or a background of neglect and abuse.

However, the first two years of life for many other children diagnosed as having A.D.H.D. have been relatively benign and "normal." In fact, although the diagnosis of A.D.H.D. is rampant, most of these children have good parents and have lived normally or near normally for the first two years of their lives. So where do all these impulse-ridden children in this epidemic come from? The parents of many children with A.D.H.D. did discipline their children while they were toddlers and ensured that their children developed basic trust during the first year. Many of these children were loving infants and responsive toddlers. It only becomes obvious that they have trouble learning, focusing, and thoughtfully carrying through on tasks when they arrive in preschool and kindergarten. So what accounts for the large number of these children with A.D.H.D. who had a good beginning in their first two years of life?

Third and Fourth Years of Development Briefly Explored

To understand the "good parent" numbers in the A.D.H.D. epidemic, the neurological development of the third and fourth years must be examined. In the 1950s, in "The Eight Stages of Man," Eric Erickson wrote about the developmental tasks of three- and four-year-old children. He noted that the tasks of the three-to-five-year-old were initiative and industry: "Now is the sense and the pervading quality of initiative. It adds to autonomy the quality of undertaking, planning and 'attacking' a task for the sake of being active and on the move. 'Initiative' there is no simpler, stronger word for it; it suggests pleasure in attack and conquest. At no time is the child more ready to learn quickly and avidly, to become bigger in the sense of sharing obligation and performance and work—identification." (Erik H. Erikson, *Childhood and Society*—second edition (Norton) "Eight Stages of Man" 255.)

Does this sound like a description of today's preschooler, kindergartner, or even first grade child? It does not! It is very rare to find small children today that stick with any task, invested in the mastery of doing something. Rarely today will one see a three-to-five-year-old working at mastering a task for more than a few minutes. Gone are the days of cutting paper dolls out of the *McCall's* magazine and dressing them with tabbed clothing. Gone are the days of making corncob dolls. Gone are the days of having a "market" in the corner of the playroom, with cans opened from the bottom so the child could "sell food" to his or her parents. Gone are the days when a toddler would be given a role of masking tape and be encouraged to completely cover a kitchen chair. Gone are most of the Tinkertoys, Erector sets, and Lincoln Logs. Gone are the days when a child would be given a cloth and be told to sew on dozens of buttons in the pattern of her choice. Gone, too, are the days of helping with household and farm tasks—gathering eggs, milking, and quilting. Gone are the days of the focus on memorizing psalms, stories, and songs at an early age.

At an essential time of brain developmental readiness for task mastery, today's three- and four-year-olds, the children who in the 1950s Erickson characterized as being at the stage of initiative and industry, are watching television and enjoying videotapes.

And therein lies the basic problem. In fact, reflecting the television and video game generation, most of the items for younger children in Toys "R" Us or any toy outlet emphasize sensory input and rudimentary motor skills, but rarely encourage creativity, task focus, job completion, or mastery. Even if they are offered for sale, Tinkertoys, Legos, Lincoln Logs, and alphabet blocks are not the big sellers. What sells big are video tapes and video games. Game Boy, Nintendo, and Playstation are the items that make millions. And of course children are exposed to more children's movies than ever before.

Today when parents "do" something with small children, it seldom involves really "doing" anything. Parents watch TV, go to a game with the children, go to the movies, or maybe, go to the zoo. Relatively rarely do today's single, dating, divorced, and commuting parents actually sit down and create or produce something with their small children. Shared focus on a mutual task may not take place at all. This was not a problem back on the farm, when there were cows to milk, eggs to gather, and pigs to slop. But it is a *definite* problem in today's world of busy parents and busy kids, who spend whatever time they do have together "relaxing."

According to the latest Nielsen figures, American preschoolers, ages two to five, watch an average of thirty hours of television weekly. That translates into 1,560 hours of television yearly, for a total of 6,240 hours by the time a typical child reaches his sixth birthday. Based on a fourteen-hour day, this means that preschoolers spend roughly one-third of their waking time watching television. In fact, it is estimated that by the time a child reaches preschool, they will have spent more time in front of a TV than they will spend throughout their entire childhood with their fathers!

Pediatrician John Rosemond notes the things a child is not doing when he is watching TV:

- Scanning
- Practicing motor skills, gross or fine
- Practicing eye-hand coordination
- Using more than two senses
- Asking questions
- Exploring

- Exercising initiative or motivation
- Being challenged
- Solving problems
- Thinking analytically
- Exercising imagination
- Practicing communication skills
- Being either creative or constructive

And these are exactly the things that children with A.D.H.D. often don't do well!

Perhaps many of today's parents, who themselves grew up in front of the TV, do not know *how* to do things with their children. Even if they know the importance of helping small children with focus and task completion, they don't know how to make a kite or a tin can telephone. They don't know how to cover chairs with masking tape, they don't know about the "corner grocery," where the child "sells" empty cans of food. They don't know about sewing on buttons with their child or making paper dolls. But most importantly, they know nothing of the developmental necessity of doing something with their preschool-aged child. They themselves grew up with Big Bird and *Sesame Street.* And now they spend time with their family going to movies and watching TV. And when their three- and four-year-old children get bored, they, as good parents, have a library of "good" videos "Disney" videos for their children to watch.

Years ago, parents were advised, if your kid is watching too much TV, be more interesting than the TV. The problem today is that many young parents, having been raised on TV themselves, are clueless about how to be more interesting than the TV. They don't know what to *do* with their kids, and so the whole family gives up and everyone sits down to *watch* something.

Indeed most "involved" parents today, encouraged by popular parenting advice, are overly concerned with *what* their child watches. Parents worry about sex and violence on TV. Some are a little concerned that their children don't watch "too much." But most are more concerned with quality than quantity, and almost none pay attention to the important aspect of the developmental age of the child who sits mesmerized in front of the TV watching *Sesame Street*—*a child at an age that two short generations ago would have been doing something, keeping himself busy, "finding something to do."*

A grandfather recently said this to me after a lecture:

"What you say about TV and a lack of internal focus is absolutely true. I have two wonderful granddaughters, one six and one four. They are active, bright kids. But you know, I noticed, even before hearing you, that after they have watched a morning of videotapes, they come out of the room, sort of floating, spacey, really. They wander aimlessly for a while. They have a lost air about them, and then they come up to me, and they say, What can I do? I told their mother that it takes them about one hour to recover from watching two videotapes. And generally these aren't spacey kids! They don't watch that much TV. But think of the poor little kids that watch it day after day!"

It is relatively rare today, even with "normal" and non-learning-disturbed children to see any child eight or younger working productively at home doing a task that takes more than a few minutes. If they are really "concentrating" for more than half an hour, it is almost certainly on TV or on a video game. When they are concentrating on something other than the TV, it is seldom a self-motivated, creative task, but much more likely to be a structured, mandatory task, such as music lessons.

Real education is dialogue!! Real education involves a feeling of mastery and the ability to respond to situations, to articulate ideas, and to respond thoughtfully. Whether we talk about leadership, creativity, responsibility, or motivation, we are describing action. Television encourages passive response. Certainly it encourages absorption and, arguably, understanding, but it does not, and cannot, by its very nature encourage doing, mastery, task completion, creativity, and independent thinking—all those things associated with being a functioning and productively busy human being. Schools must by their nature focus on doing and task completion.

Today, so many children have problems with task completion that some educators simply give up and go back to entertaining the kids. They read stories, show videotapes, take field trips, and in other ways consciously or unconsciously focus on passive learning. As one teacher succinctly put it, "The kids are good at sitting there and looking at me...They think I'm a TV. I do think they are actually absorbing some of the things I'm saying, but it's hard to be sure, because they can only prove it by articulating concepts or completing a paper, and that's something no TV program expects...So the kids are at sort of a loss there."

Unconsciously, across the social spectrum, there is progressively less expectation that children do something. For instance, across the nation, schools and churches offer night classes for adults and parents, with child care provided. Care to guess what the "child care" consists of? That's right, showing the kids a videotape. No church or synagogue "child care room" is complete without the ubiquitous VCR and monitor. Gone are the days when child care consisted of teaching children poetry or songs or focusing on an evening task.

The sheer amount of time small children sit in front of a TV cannot be overestimated. It is generally believed that most small children spend more time in front of the TV than they spend with their parents or other adults doing something in child care. Truthfully, about the only place children now actually do something is at Sunday school, where they paste pictures of Jesus and lambs made of cotton on pieces of paper. It is generally in such formalized situations—Sunday school, music lessons, dance lessons, and, of course, school—that children might actually be expected to do something. When children have free, nonstructured time, most can be found in front of the TV. Rarely will a child make something at home that merits being put on the refrigerator.

Recently, a businessman and his wife, fed up with the amount of time their elementary age children sat in front of the TV, bet the children $200 apiece that they could not go one year without watching TV in the home. The kids took the parents up on the bet. And they won. To the parents' amazement, after the year was up, the children asked the parents not to return the TV to the home. The kids had found, over the year, that it was just too much fun to be doing things with their parents and in a self-motivated way. They realized that they had been missing out on some important things.

Even when the "critical periods" theory is taken into account, we cannot say that all children who don't learn to focus, concentrate, and master a task during the third and fourth years are doomed to never learn these skills. However, I believe strongly that these children grow up under a definite handicap, and it is much more difficult to learn to focus, create, and achieve a sense of mastery in later years.

The crux of the situation is that by the time they start school, millions of American children are already developmentally impoverished, and they show it with impulsive behavior, inability to focus, lack of task mastery, and poor follow-through. And sometimes they are diagnosed with A.D.H.D. or as having a "learning problem."

A college basketball coach recalls that the players he led a generation ago read books on the bus to pass the time. Today, they don their Walkman headphones and break out their Gameboys. For years, the coach diagramed plays on a blackboard, representing opposing players with Xs and Os. More recently, however, he has begun noticing that the athletes do not understand the plays unless he shows them videos of the teams in action. "The kids have changed over the years," he says. "They seem to have lost their abstract thinking skills."

And most have developed the problem because of impoverished, developmentally inappropriate first, second, third, and fourth years of life.

Although the causes of A.D.H.D. are multiple and A.D.H.D. exists as a part of many disorders, the shear numbers of children now being given this diagnosis—apparently accurately—would lead any thoughtful person to wonder what could be going on in the *culture itself* that could cause such an epidemic.

chapter seven

Why Kids with Attention Problems Need Love and Logic: Two Stories

When Jonathan was born, his parents looked at him with awe. One of God's miracles was theirs to love and raise. They wanted to do everything right. Jonathan seemed happy and healthy. Maybe they were a little indulgent, but who wouldn't indulge such a beautiful child?

He became a fussy eater, but they didn't mind. Jonathan might throw a bowl of food onto the floor if he didn't like it, but they could always find some food he would eat.

He was a bit of a rascal when other children came over to play. One time he bit another child and they tried to send him to his room. Jonathan became quite upset, and his parents had to ask their neighbor to take her child home. It took almost an hour to calm Jonathan down.

When he was four, they hoped a preschool experience would help Jonathan develop social skills. He seemed very bright and precocious, but preschool didn't work out. Jonathan was disruptive and sometimes aggressive. He took other children's toys and began to defy the teacher when she interfered. Jonathan just didn't seem to click with her. After Christmas, his parents decided he'd had enough preschool.

At a doctor's appointment for an ear infection, Jonathan's mother asked about his difficulty playing with other children. It was beginning to concern her. She said Jonathan was still a picky eater. He really liked macaroni and cheese and chicken nuggets. She could sometimes get him to eat vegetables by using candy or dessert as a reward. And, he was beginning to be a TV junkie. He really enjoyed cartoons and Disney movies. The physician reassured Jonathan's mother that he was developing normally, but suggested that they should monitor his success in school.

Kindergarten didn't go so well, and that's when his parents began to investigate A.D.H.D. Jonathan didn't like the teacher, and some of the other kids were mean and wouldn't play with him. He could concentrate on a TV show or a video game, but could not remember to pick up his toys or turn off the video. By first grade, he was taking Ritalin twice a day.

Things seemed a little better. His listening skills improved, and a couple of the boys in class would play with him. Jonathan was still kind of clumsy and didn't write his name well. He couldn't skip or do jumping jacks, but he loved to run. He joined a soccer team and had fun, even though he usually didn't seem to know where the ball was.

Jonathan received special help in reading during second grade, but other than that, the school was not very cooperative. Right before Christmas, he was suspended for part of a day when he spit in another child's face and then ran away from the principal when she tried to discipline him. How could the principal not see how excited he was about Christmas? Unfair!

In third grade, Jonathan was referred to special education but didn't qualify as learning disabled. He wasn't getting his work done at school. His parents talked to the doctor about upping his medication, but decided to wait. His mother picked him up each day in order to get a list of assignments that were not completed and also to keep him off the bus, where problems had also developed.

Jonathan's mom spent hours with him every day after school, and by the time he was in middle school, she was getting tired of it. Her beautiful boy was getting bigger. He didn't enjoy school. He and his friends were starting to act rebellious at times. He refused to bring home his assignment book, so she couldn't help him complete his work. She made an appointment with the principal, and on that particular day, Jonathan was caught, apparently holding some cigarettes for another boy. When his mom went in for her appointment, the principal said he wanted to suspend Jonathan. She talked him out of it, but that night Jonathan didn't come home until eight o'clock. He said he'd been at Eric's house, but of course he hadn't. She knew because she had called to check. His mother cried that night as she made Jonathan something to eat. In her heart, she knew she and her husband had taken a wrong path with their son. But the right path wasn't clear, and she didn't know what to do.

• • • • •

Nick's parents realized right away that they were facing a challenge. They received him from the adoption agency when he was only a week old. He was still small, but spunky. He slept restlessly, and as a result, so did they. Formula was a problem for him. They had to switch from cow's milk, and even soy caused him to suffer from gas and bloating after awhile. They were glad when he was old enough for cereals and baby foods but had to watch carefully to see which foods caused him to develop diaper rash or get especially cranky.

He was only eighteen months old when they knew their parenting skills were going to need some support if they were going to live calmly with Nick. That's when they began the process of trying to incorporate Love and Logic into their lives.

They tried to cut down on the anger and the "no, no, no's" when they disciplined Nick. It took a few tries before he accepted the notion of "recovery time." His blue eyes flashed angrily at them when they calmly carried him to his room for his first time-out. In a few minutes, his tirade ceased, and they waited a couple more minutes before welcoming him back to their company.

Nick was truly a busy boy. He moved and played and moved and played. His tendency to develop ear infections was mitigated by their careful attention to avoiding mucous-causing foods in his diet. They set up a great play area in the basement where he could run and swing and play on a balance beam.

When he was three, Nick's folks put him into preschool three mornings a week. This coincided with the arrival of their second child, which made Nick a little anxious. He had a great need for physical movement, which the preschool readily offered. After Maria was born, Nick tested the limits of behavior a few times. The teacher had to put him into recovery time, but he calmed down quickly and asked if he could come out if he was nice.

Nick became a great little four-year-old helper at home. He and his dad would rake leaves in the yard for hours, and Nick would jump into the pile and they'd have to rake them again. Sometimes they'd work together in the garage.

"What tools do you think we're going to use?" his dad would ask. "Do you think we should draw up a plan, or just start building before we have a plan?"

When a job was almost done, his dad would ask, "Do you think we should clean up this mess now or just wait till next week? I'll bet we will feel proud when we've got the whole job done. Let's clean up!"

In this way, Nick began learning thinking skills that were particularly valuable to him, because he was intrinsically impulsive. (If his parents had known about the alcoholism and other substance abuse in Nick's genetic history, they might never have adopted him.) Sometimes it took great effort to follow through on a consequence and let Nick feel the pain of his own decisions. When he was six, he threw a rock through the neighbor's stained-glass window. Insurance paid for most of it, but Nick had to pay the $250 deductible. He drained his bank account of $218, and the remaining $32 came from the sale of his favorite Lone Ranger audiotape collection. His parents were so sad.

When he was seven, Nick forgot to put on his helmet one day when his friend David came over to ride bikes. It wasn't long before he saw his bike hanging from the garage ceiling.

"When am I going to get it back?" he begged his mom.

"I don't know, sweetheart," she replied. "I guess when I'm not afraid you're going to be forgetting your helmet anymore."

For days afterward, Nick's mom cried when she went into the garage, but she resisted the urge to give Nick's bike back to him immediately.

In third grade, Nick forgot to return his school permission slip so he could go on a field trip to the zoo. His mother had signed it, but somehow he had misplaced it between taking it off the table and putting it in his backpack. With a less-impulsive child, a child who could use less energy and still maintain attention to important details, his parents might have bailed him out. But Nick was not such a child. They knew his tendency to inattention or impulse, and they knew he needed to experience a real-world consequence to help him learn to make the extra effort to be responsible. Nick stayed at school in another classroom while his classmates went to the zoo.

By fourth grade, the homework was starting to come in earnest. His parents helped Nick choose a study place and a study time, and then his father made him an offer. "I'd be willing to give you half an hour of help any night you ask for it. Fair enough?"

"Sure," said Nick.

"And if you need me to help you longer than thirty minutes or to supervise you to make sure your work is getting done, what should happen then?"

"What do you mean?"

"I mean the first thirty minutes is free because I love you, but if I need to spend more time than that, it takes away from my family time or from my rest. So what should happen?"

"I guess if I use more time than half an hour, I'll have to make it up to you."

"You guessed right," said Nick's dad.

Nick laughed. "You mean I'll have to do some of your chores to make up the time?"

"Right again," said Nick's dad, with a smile of love for his boy.

Children with challenging behaviors or attentional challenges are capable of learning, and Nick's parents always held to the belief that he could be responsible for his choices. And they held to a vision and a plan that increased the odds that Nick would make the extra effort required to become a responsible adult.

······❤······

More Ideas for Parents to Consider

This chapter is for the parents of every child who has difficulty sustaining attention. Rich or poor, medicated or not medicated, labeled or unlabeled, children with attention problems all present different needs. Some solutions presented in this chapter apply to most children with attention problems. Other solutions apply more selectively. It is our hope that you will experiment to see which solutions work best for you.

For best results use the ideas in this chapter after you have begun to make progress on any major behavioral issues at home.

The ideas in this chapter are gathered from many sources. Some are scientifically validated as useful (for some children). Others are derived from scores of parent interviews or from the experience of therapists, physicians, and teachers.

My suggestion is that you make a log of ideas you wish to try. Consider the cost of certain ideas and the time commitment required. Consider that some of these suggestions require parents to develop new skills or priorities. Try to involve your child in the process as much as possible. And work slowly. Don't try every strategy that interests you at once. Pick one or two at a time. Try them carefully, for at least two to four weeks, then evaluate them for effectiveness. At that point, you can either consider how you might incorporate a specific strategy into your lifestyle, or choose to discard it.

With all of the ideas presented here, we assume that you are using Love and Logic techniques with your child at home to help him develop problem-solving skills and a clear awareness that there are natural or logical consequences to his choices. We also hope and pray that you have chosen to develop positive relationships with the adults who work with your child at school so that you will have a partnership and a network of support.

Develop Patterns of Home and Schoolwork Organization

Most children with attentional difficulties need more routines in their lives. Routines become habits of attention and links to helpful behaviors.

A morning routine may include a regular waking time, plenty of time for a shower and breakfast, making the bed, some quiet music, a regular place where backpack or books were stored the night before, and time to pack a lunch or chat with family. A child or adult with fewer impulsive tendencies has a lesser need for routine. Variance may not affect them or cause them to forget to prepare for the day. But kids who can't organize their thinking or behavior easily need routines.

An after-school routine might include snack, exercise, and then quiet time before dinner. After dinner might include family chores and study time in a regular place. Using study time well might require instruction. Reviewing your daily planner, establishing priorities, finishing each assignment before going on to the next, and reviewing what's likely to happen tomorrow are habits and skills that take practice. A bedtime routine may include bath, stories or conversation, quiet reading, relaxing music, prayer or meditation, along with a regular time for your child to be quietly in his room.

At a parenting workshop, a concerned mother urgently raised her hand to ask a question. "Do you mean that if I want to help my son,

I'm going to have to get my own life more organized as well?" she asked
with concern.

"It's certainly possible," I answered. "Can you tell me more about the
model of organization you present at home?"

"I'm artistic," she explained. "We don't have regular meals or bed-
times, if that's what you mean."

She was thinking as she was talking. "Oh, God," she said. "I can see
what I have to do, but it won't be easy."

In the modern age of busy lifestyles, it might not be easy. You might
want to start with the basics, including a regular study time and place
(to be used for quiet reading even if your child has no homework that
day), use of an assignment book, a regular bedtime routine, and a system
for knowing where all schoolwork can be found.

Chores

The home program clearly describes the importance of chores in the
life of your child. Fifty years ago it was easier to help kids feel valued.
They had jobs that were necessary for the welfare, or even the survival,
of the family. "If nobody gathers the eggs," said one wise mother,
"there's not going to be any breakfast."

Packaged foods, modern conveniences, and the misrepresentation
of family life that is shown in the media make it easy to overlook the
value of chores. Sometimes it's just easier for parents to take care of
household tasks themselves.

Chores teach persistence. Chores help kids feel valued. Chores remind
us that we are not alone. Chores build loyalty. Chores build work skills
and, occasionally, teamwork. Chores help us begin to understand that
service to others is one of life's great rewards.

Some parents make a list of adult chores and child chores, then help
the kids sort out their choices.

Some parents make a list with the help of their children of all the
chores it takes to keep the family going. Adult chores might include
paying the bills and driving kids to soccer practice. The family sits

down together to divide up the chores, with parents taking the usual adult responsibilities and some of the other household duties. The children begin to claim chores of their own. Some of their chores might include making dinner on Thursday, taking out the garbage, clearing dishes, making beautiful pictures for the house, and singing songs for their parents.

Some parents are willing to put a list of the adult chores they'd be willing to hire some child to do on the refrigerator door. Sometimes they take bids. Of course, the basic chores a child has chosen are not for pay. Chores are a part of being in the family and taking care of the family.

Medication

Whether to medicate is a difficult choice for some parents, and not one we hope to solve for you in this book. If you do choose to use medication, consider the following ideas:

- Find a doctor who listens carefully and will work with you. Today, there are several options when considering medication. Talk about them with your doctor.
- Using Ritalin, then observing your child to see if he is calmer or stays on-task better, is not a reasonable way to diagnose whether your child has an attention deficit. Ritalin and other amphetamines are performance enhancers. Most kids or adults will stay focused better if they use these drugs. The use of Ritalin should not in itself be diagnostic. Work with a professional who will help you gather data about the degree of attention problems your child may have before a diagnosis is made.
- Once a medication is prescribed, monitor target behaviors carefully at home and at school. Watch for side effects. Many doctors will carefully adjust dosage or delivery after reviewing this information with you.

Early Stimulation

In her wonderful book *Endangered Minds* (Touchstone, 1990), Jane Healy looks at the modern environment most children experience and concludes that language skills, thinking skills, problem solving, and attentional skills are not being developed to their potential. Poor language models, overuse of videos and computer games as language teachers and baby-sitters, lack of interactive play, and infrequent modeling of thinking and attentional processes all contribute to this concern.

Of course it is likely that children who have experienced less nurturing and less appropriately stimulating environments will have difficulty developing attention skills. Then they come to school. Veteran teachers observe the differences between today's kindergarten and first grade classes and those of twenty years ago. Kids have changed. For all our fancy technology and wealth, many children are coming to school less ready to learn and with poorer attention skills. National studies confirm it. Advertisers know it. Messages are packed into shorter bits and repeated more often.

Consider the irony. In a time when medical knowledge and information regarding brain growth and development, how kids learn, and effective parenting practices are more available than ever before, more kids are having problems. If your children are young, or as yet unborn, the following suggestions for enriching their early environment may help you and your child:

- At birth, the brain is remarkably unfinished. Around 100 billion nerve cells, or neurons, each with the potential to establish hundreds of neuronal connections, await the experiences that will cause this small brain to develop further.
- Warmth, love, and touch are early needs. Nursing provides healthy food along with touch experiences and the development of sucking patterns important to further development. The skin is the largest organ of the body, and so important to early development. Healthy touch encourages early brain growth, as does sound stimulation

like talking and beautiful music. Vision begins to develop with an early awareness of the contrast between dark and light, and later an attraction to red and other bright colors.

• Reading and singing to your child are appropriate at any age. Playful responses to facial expressions, gestures, and sounds begin the process of interactive communication and help the child begin to develop attentional skills. Routines at bedtime, bath, and meals help the child begin to recognize sequence and wonder what comes next.

• Physical movement further develops the infant's brain. Pressure on the proprioceptors at each joint creates awareness of body position. As the baby raises her head to look for toys or friendly humans, she stimulates an awareness of balance—tenuous at first and gradually better as she learns to move her head and later her body. With the experience of crawling and creeping, the baby develops the ability to coordinate body movement, including the coordination of right and left sides. These movement experiences create an integration of function between the right and left hemispheres of the brain, which lay the foundation for sophisticated thinking processes.

• With balance and movement comes the integration of visual processes with physical movement. Gross-motor skills lay the foundation for fine-motor skills and visual-motor skills, like cutting, coloring, drawing, manipulation of small objects, and playing with Legos, clay, and puzzles.

• Play becomes an important learning experience. Miraculously, kids are drawn to the kinds of play experiences that are exactly suitable to their own brain growth and development. The child who builds a tower and knocks it down over and over is developing the visual-motor skills and awareness of form constancy that he needs at his particular phase of development. The child who loves to spin is stimulating balance processes. The child who asks "why?" is stimulating listening skill development, language use skills, predictability skills, and social skills.

• In the right environment, kids are drawn to activities that are perfect for their brain development. And then there is TV.

> *Hours of video viewing do not develop good language skills.*
> **Only interactive language does that.** *Hours of video viewing do not develop good visual or visual-memory skills.* **Only interactive experience with objects you can touch and move and talk about does that.** *Hours of videos or computer games do not develop attentional skills.* **Only interactive experiences that require persistence and occasionally struggle will help develop attention.**

Physical safety, warmth, good nutrition, beautiful sounds, interesting things to look at, move and manipulate, opportunities for balance and physical movement, a few toys to manipulate and spark imagination, interactive language and play, very little TV, even more movement and talking and touch add up to a nurturing environment where kids's brains will grow and develop.

Cardiovascular Exercise

American children are fatter and have less physical endurance and more heart health risk factors than ever before. Could this be related to attention?

In the previous section of this chapter, there was a reference to the importance of early movement experiences for brain growth and development. Patterns of activity, fat-to-muscle ratio, and cardiovascular health are also affected by early experience.

Cardiovascular health and activity can be lifelong allies for children and adults with attention problems. The research has been clear for decades. Students who engage in cardiovascular activities like walking, biking, rope skipping, jogging, aerobics, cross-country skiing, or sustained swimming demonstrate improved behaviors, better attention, and more learning. Of course, the same is true for adults.

Cardiovascular exercise is not just a way to release extra energy and feel physically capable. Specific hormonal and neurochemical changes occur when you sustain cardiovascular exercise and raise your heart rate for more than fifteen or twenty minutes. These changes improve attentional states and moods in ways that are remarkably similar to the use of stimulant or antidepressive medications.

Parents who find an enjoyable cardiovascular activity to practice with a child who has attention problems could improve attention, increase self-esteem, reduce depression, improve fitness, reduce heart-health risk factors, improve sleep and appetite, and have a good time. Consider daily walks, running, bicycling, swimming, or sports that require sustained effort. It might be good for the kid as well.

Martial Arts/Physical Discipline

I don't like lousy Kung-Fu movies either, but try to put away your pre-judgment. For some children, participation in martial arts or similarly demanding physical disciplines may be a wonderful way to develop self-control and respect for others. These disciplines may help children with attention problems in many ways. They train children to learn how to manage their physical and mental energy in a focused way. They teach patterns of attention. Breathing, posture, movement, and attitude must combine in harmony for a student to be successful. Kids feel good about themselves as they improve their physical coordination. They practice rituals of respect. They have an acceptable opportunity to handle aggressive feelings without hurting others.

There are many differences in the martial arts taught in this country. Karate teaches intense concentration, defensive blocks, and kicking or striking techniques. Judo comes from a Chinese word meaning "gentle way." It emphasizes throwing one's opponent and knowing how to use pressure on the body. Aikido teaches defensive-style techniques and the redirection of your opponent's energy. Tae Kwon Do is a Korean style of karate that emphasizes kicking. Kenpo combines martial arts with traditional boxing. Tai Chi is a noncontact slow motion discipline.

If your child expresses interest in the martial arts, look carefully for an appropriate program and instructor. Many local recreation programs offer classes. Don't hesitate to ask about the instructor's certification and to observe a lesson or two before enrolling.

Balance

Andrew was a five-year-old red-haired ball of kindergarten energy. His teacher didn't call for help because she was concerned about his balance. She called to save her sanity.

He moved around the room, pausing briefly at activity centers, knocking over projects and occasionally other children. He sat toward the back of the group at story time for about ten seconds before he began rolling, then wandering around the back of the room. He cocked his head and seemed to look out of the sides of his eyes as he roamed. He noticed me watching him, but never looked directly at me.

He couldn't stand still in line. He bumped forward and backward. An aide tried to corral him as the class marched down to the gymnasium, but he got away. She headed him back.

Andrew couldn't follow directions well in P.E., even though he was trying. He moved away if a ball came near.

His mother told me about behavior problems at home and about the incessant movement. He'd been expelled from two preschools. She also told me about the chronic ear infections he had experienced between the ages of two and four.

Andrew needed a big dose of Love and Logic at home, but that wasn't all he needed. Andrew couldn't comfortably stand still. He wobbled when he got tired. He certainly wasn't comfortable sitting still, which takes good balance and the ability to inhibit large muscle activity. His gross-motor skills weren't too bad, but he'd never been able to sit or stand still long enough to develop fine-motor or visual-motor skills. He couldn't color or draw or cut with scissors. He was visually disoriented because his two visual spheres were not well integrated. He couldn't judge distance well and consequently ran into things a lot. He kind of felt his way around the room.

If she hadn't been so desperate, his mother never would have tried the Love and Logic or the balance exercises at home or given time and attention to building his gross-motor and fine-motor skills. If she hadn't been so desperate, she never would have worked so hard to monitor his diet to remove foods that might cause mucus buildup and contribute to his balance problems.

She didn't cry at all during our first meeting. It wasn't until a few months later as we sat down to reevaluate his home program that she burst into tears. They had visited family at the holidays. He hadn't been perfect, but he sat at the table, and he listened when Grandma spoke to him, and she knew now that her son could have a future.

Balance problems are not the same as attention problems. But the development of balance is related to the development of motor skills, listening skills, visual spatial skills, visual processing, and visual memory. Minimal balance skills are necessary for all these to develop.

If a first grade boy is sitting in his chair giving much of his energy to keeping himself from falling on the floor (you'd be surprised how often this happens), he has less energy and attention to give to the teacher or the book or the lesson. Helping your child develop automatic balance skills (that means balance without having to think about it) will help him have fewer distractions and less difficulty sustaining attention for difficult tasks.

Every child deserves the opportunity to develop good balance. Lots of physical play, outside games, rhythmic movement, avoidance of allergies and ear infections, gymnastics, and great P.E. programs in preschools and schools will help children develop good balance. Kids with attention problems don't need additional challenges to keep them from being successful.

Sensory Integration

A preschool teacher once asked me, "Do any of these other children have sensory integration needs?"

I looked around the room. Two little girls were playing at the water table. They were pouring water back and forth from one container to another. Sometimes a little bit spilled.

Four boys were in the block area. They independently built block structures. Trying to step around their classmates's structures was difficult at times. They planned their buildings. They moved their bodies as carefully as they could.

Three of the children were painting, wearing plastic bibs down to their knees. They looked at the large blocks of paper and planned their designs, then tried to manipulate brush and color to resemble an idea or object. Sometimes I could even tell what they were painting.

As I scanned the purposeful activity around the room, it was clear to me that play is truly the business of childhood, and most play directly contributes to the building of complex sensory-motor skills. Each time a child feels the shape of a building block while examining it with his eyes, then plans how to use it, holds large muscles steady, creates stable balance, uses fine muscles to move and adjust the object, then gets up to find another piece for his construction project without stumbling and knocking the whole edifice down, he is engaged in a miraculously complex sensory-integrative function. Developing, organizing, and integrating movement, balance, sight, sound, and touch is the complex business of childhood.

All young children have sensory integration needs. A few have severe needs. Some overreact to touch. Others experience great difficulty judging where their bodies are in space and frequently bump and fall. Still others have difficulty tuning out extraneous sounds or activity so they can concentrate on one task at a time.

Some kids need extra help.

While most children can get the greatest benefit from stimulating play environments and lots of physical movement, the neediest children may need help with early sensory-motor development from a skilled therapist. Some, but not all, occupational therapists are trained for this work. Ask about their areas of special training or certification. Consider taking the time to observe any therapist you are thinking about hiring to work with your child.

Visual or Auditory Process Training

Most school systems have teachers of speech and language who are well trained to work with young children. They evaluate a child's ability to produce normal speech sounds, but also evaluate a child's listening memory, ability to distinguish specific sounds, ability to blend sounds, and ability to listen in a distracting environment. Sometimes they'll evaluate basic hearing acuity. By working with young children, they help many overcome minor difficulties before a problem significantly interferes with school success.

Unfortunately, visual processing difficulties are more likely to go unnoticed. Most teachers are not specifically trained to notice whether a child has difficulty with depth perception, maintaining eye-teaming within near point (the reach of your hand), visual tracking, or visual memory.

Today, more children than in the past seem to come to school with less-developed visual-motor, visual processing, and visual-memory skills. Thousands of hours of passive video watching, childhood illnesses, including ear infection and allergy, and a lack of early motor-skill development certainly contribute to the likelihood of young children coming to school with poorly developed visual skills. School systems, for all their good intentions, sometimes make matters worse for these children. Asking a child with poor hand-eye coordination to accurately copy long printing assignments leads to frustration. While a little bit of frustration is fine, sustained expectation of failure is not fine.

Asking a child with lousy visual-memory skills to recognize whole words she has seen only a few times before may also be detrimental. She may begin to over-rely on auditory decoding skills if her visual memory consistently fails her.

Asking a child who must strain his eyes and use great effort to see one clear image using his two visual fields may lead to avoidance of reading tasks, watery eyes, occluding (blocking) one visual field, and fatigue.

Encouraging stimulating early play opportunities and motor-skill development, placing restrictions on TV and computer game time, and providing early reading programs that allow the skills of early reading to develop at different times (within the first few grades) for different children are enough for most kids. Occasionally, a child with more significant visual-processing delays may need the assistance of a developmentally trained optometrist or ophthalmologist.

Nutrition and Allergies

Once the subject of speculation and incomplete science, the relationships between nutrition and attention, and also between allergies and attention for many children, have now been well established.

Most of this isn't rocket science. When Jimmy wakes up late, rolls into his clothes, and grabs a Mountain Dew on his way to the school bus, don't expect him to think well during his morning classes. The value of good nutrition for all of us has been well established. The value of good nutrition for children who are at risk of attention and learning problems is especially worth our attention.

A healthy breakfast, reasonable limits on the use of refined sugars, lots of fresh fruits and vegetables, and a varied diet can be recommended for all. Doctors and nutritionists may argue over the specifics of a plan to use nutritional supplements, but don't wait around for a unanimous opinion. The use of multiple vitamins, antioxidants, colloidal minerals, digestive enzymes, and specific amino acids have been recommended by researchers in the last few years. My own assessment of the research tells me that no single approach is the right approach for all children with attention problems. Consult your most trusted healthcare professional and consider developing a nutritional plan.

Allergens in the environment and in the food are also a factor for some children. As a special education classroom teacher, I observed and noted the puffy eyes, dark circles under the eyes, sinus drainage, stuffy nose, stomachaches, and headaches that some of my students experienced daily. I also noted the behavior changes some of them experienced after lunch or a snack, and the cravings these students had for specific foods.

William Crook, Doris Rapp, Lendon Smith, C. Keith Conners, and others have noted the relationship between food sensitivities and the attention problems of some children. Common allergens include cow's milk (and milk products), chocolate, wheat, grapes, soy products, peanuts, corn, sugar, and oranges.

Some allergies are easy to spot, but many food allergies have a subtler range of symptoms, including irritability, hyperactivity, fatigue, difficulty concentrating, diminished visual-motor skills, stuffy nose, dark circles under the eyes, puffy eyes, headaches, and gas.

If you suspect your child is sensitive to certain foods, consult your doctor or begin by reading books by any of the authors referenced in this section. Some doctors recommend allergy testing. Others may suggest an elimination diet. That is, a diet that removes common or suspected allergens for one to two weeks, or until your child's symptoms improve. A careful record of diet and symptoms is kept, then suspected foods are reintroduced one at a time as you carefully note reactions. Learn more about this process before beginning on your own.

Changing your child's eating habits can be tough. We tend to crave the foods to which we have become sensitive.

I'll never forget Calvin. He was a skinny bean who was impulsive, hyperactive, and smart. For two years, I observed his frequent trips to his locker. He always had a great explanation. It was another student who finally ratted on him.

One day, I gave him permission to go to his locker, then I sneaked around the other way to observe him. The hallway was quiet. He looked around, opened his locker, then looked again. Confident that he was unobserved, Calvin brought out the half-gallon juice container full of white sugar and began to pour it into his mouth. He gulped and swallowed and continued to pour. He surely swallowed at least two cups of sugar before he sighed deeply and returned his beloved sugar to the locker.

During his feeding, I had walked twenty yards down the hallway and was now standing beside him. He hadn't noticed me until that moment, and I observed the additional sugar containers in his locker.

For two years, I had worked with this boy. I knew his family and had visited his home on several occasions. I thought I knew him, but realized at that moment how little I knew about the importance of his diet and how significantly his food choices were affecting his success in school and in life.

The Power of Expectations

As a student teacher at Willow Run High School back in 1970, I had two mentally impaired students in a general social studies class. I only knew about one. The friendly red-haired girl looked different, and I realized that she was mentally slow. Wanda usually turned in work that was less organized, not well presented, and often messy. I reinforced her for her efforts and her friendly smile. Not until the end of the course did I realize what a dunce I was.

All semester a tall, quiet boy had been sitting next to her. On several occasions Alan turned in sloppy work or poorly developed answers. I promptly gave them back and told him I expected more from him, and Alan resubmitted much-improved assignments.

On the last day of the semester, I walked to the old Type A special education classroom to say good-bye to the teacher. My friendly redhead was there, and also, to my great surprise, was tall, quiet Alan. He handed me a letter without saying anything. It was one of those letters that make you want to dedicate your life to teaching. In his letter, Alan told me how much I'd helped him grow. He thanked me for never giving up on him.

Wanda smiled as I left the room and the teacher followed me out into the hall. He'd noticed my surprise, and I showed him my letter. He explained to me that Alan's I.Q. scores were lower than Wanda's, and he laughed with me about how I hadn't known and had placed higher expectations on this quiet retarded boy.

It took me a long time to fully realize what I'd done. My own lack of knowledge had caused me to give a precious gift to one, but not another.

Robert Rosenthal conducted a series of experiments in the 1960s and 1970s in which he tested the effect of expectations. He later called this the Pygmalion effect. Rosenthal showed that teacher expectation clearly affected student performance. He later demonstrated that student expectation of teacher performance also affected student achievement. (Be careful how you talk about your child's teacher!)

As I write this segment, it is evening. The kids are laughing upstairs, and someone is taking a bath, and I'm reflecting on a third grade boy I evaluated this morning. He was wonderful, smart, and charming. Last year he was prescribed and took Ritalin, but he had frequent headaches and the medication was discontinued. He has terrible visual-processing problems, but that's for another chapter.

We finished our work and sat talking. He asked me if I knew he had A.D.D.

"Someone told me about that," I answered. "And you told me about the Ritalin."

"That's why I get into trouble," he explained.

"What?"

"The A.D.D. When people are talking, I just can't keep my mouth shut, and I just jump right in. It's because I have A.D.D."

One of the realities about A.D.H.D. is that expectations define reality. Whether it's by our words, body language, or thoughts, we share the content of our expectations with the children we know. Some children receive messages that they are capable of making good choices, responsible for their decisions, likely to have a wonderful life, and will be worthy of our love forever. Some children don't.

Attribution Theory

Two students are waiting in class as their tests are being returned.

They sit near each other, but have a different view on the experience that is coming.

Mark gets his test results first. Seventy-five percent, he groans to himself. He's embarrassed and not looking forward to sharing the test results with others. He forgot to take his books home the night before the test, he remembers. He watches the teacher as she finishes distributing the graded tests. She notices his look and smiles. I'd better get it in gear, he thinks. This may not be my favorite class, but if I work harder for the next month, I'll still be in good shape.

Stanley takes his test without looking at the teacher. This sucks, he thinks as he looks at the grade—seventy-five percent. This class is boring and the teacher is boring. How was I supposed to know there was going to be a test? The teacher never even checked to see if I had written the assignment down in the notebook she gave me. She hates me anyway. I'll never do well in a school like this, where the courses suck and the teachers hate kids.

· · · · ·

Attribution Theory examines the causes to which people attribute success and failure in their lives. In this example, Mark attributes his grade to his own forgetfulness and decides he has the ability to make up for this mistake by future effort.

Stanley attributes his problem to the teacher for not checking more carefully to see if he's using his assignment notebook. He has no specific plans for doing better by improving his own effort.

In one case, a boy decides that he's responsible for a poor performance and capable of doing better by showing more effort. In the other case, a boy decides someone else is responsible for his poor performance. He feels helpless and inadequate to change his future.

To what do we attribute our successes and failures? Last summer, I brought in a huge pile of fresh vegetables and washed them in the sink. I cut off the extra leaves and pushed them into the garbage disposal. I packaged the vegetables and put them away in the refrigerator. As a last step, I cleaned up the sink, washed the last bits of leaf and sand down the drain and turned on the disposal. It whirred smoothly for about a second, then clanked and clattered. I reached for the switch and turned it off.

I knew what I had done, but resisted knowing and tried the switch again. A terrible noise came from the disposal. In my mind, I searched for another explanation for wrecking the disposal besides the one I knew to be true. But no one else was home. No kids had distracted my thoughts. My wife hadn't asked me to clean the veggies. It was me. I was forced to attribute my problem to my decision to let sand accumulate in the disposal. I would have to either fix the disposal or buy a new one.

By teaching us to use empathy, Love and Logic helps us avoid giving kids the opportunity to blame others for their mistakes.

"Dad, I'm so hungry."

"I know sweetie. That's what happens to me when I don't eat enough for breakfast. But don't worry. At noon we'll get a great lunch."

• • • • •

"Mom, I can't find any clean clothes that I want to wear."

"Bummer. What are you going to do?"

"But Mom, you haven't washed any of my clothes all week."

"I know, sweetheart. I only wash clothes that are put in the laundry, and I noticed that yours are piled up in your closet."

"It's not fair."

"I know."

"All I have left to wear is that ugly green shirt Grandma gave me."

"That's sad," stated with true empathy. "What are you going to do?"

"I guess I'll be doing my own wash tonight."

• • • • •

"David won't play with me."

"That's sad. What are you going to do?"

"Don't you want to know why?"

"Sure. I'd be glad to listen."

• • • • •

Love and Logic helps us hold our children accountable for their decisions without stealing their opportunity to learn by ranting, raving, and lecturing. We hope that our kids will learn that most of their mistakes and achievements are based on their own abilities, efforts, and decisions. We also hope they'll come to appreciate mistakes as wonderful opportunities to learn.

Some parents and teachers have used specific noticing to reinforce positive attributions.

Children with attention problems, like all other children, will improve their self-worth and be far more successful if they develop a sense of ownership and responsibility for the events that transpire in their lives.

Specific noticing is different than general praise, which uses nice, but nonspecific words in an attempt to reinforce behavior: "Good job." "Nice try." "You're great."

There's nothing wrong with general praise if it's used occasionally, but children don't learn much from it, and sometimes it sounds insincere. Specific noticing points out the relationship between a particular act or acts and a positive outcome. It's especially powerful when you help your child think about how she did something well.

Good: "Your posture was good and your voice was clear throughout your speech."

Better: "Your posture was good and your voice was clear. How did you maintain that?"

Good: "I noticed you were listening well today."

Better: "I noticed you were listening well today. How did you stay focused that long?"

Good: "Great backhand position on that last shot."

Better: "Great backhand position on that last shot. How did you learn that so quickly?"

Sometimes specific noticing builds relationships as well, because you've communicated that you have noticed something special about another person:

"No one has ever asked that question in all the years I've taught this class. It's a thoughtful question, and I thank you."

"That's a great looking coat you have on. It matches your eyes."

"Your use of descriptive language was remarkable. You clearly care about the place you were describing."

Another technique that works well in business, in the classroom or at home is the use of "What's Working Well" meetings. Some executives begin important meetings by asking everyone in a department or on project team to describe what's working well. This gives them an opportunity to ask questions like, "How did you come up with that idea?" or "What made your idea work?" or "How did you get so many people to cooperate?" Questions like this give team members a chance to attach positive outcomes to the characteristics of the team or its members.

Teachers can use similar tactics in classroom meetings or adapt the strategy to meetings with individual students. "What's going well for you in this class?" "You seem pretty organized. How do you manage that?" "In this science project, you developed a unique theory. Can you tell me about your thinking process?" Questions like this help students discover how they did something well.

Creating Powerful People Through Specific Noticing

Parents can schedule regular review meetings for ten minutes once or twice a week, with the clear purpose of reviewing schoolwork or home projects their child has done well. "Tell me how you knew what to study for this test." "What steps did you take to organize your thoughts for this report? It's remarkably well organized." "How do you remember all the different assignments from six different teachers?" "Will you show me something you're especially proud of from this past week?"

Here's one more sneaky little method. Notice specific positive behaviors or characteristics when your kids think you don't know they're listening. Kids will remember what they think they were not supposed to hear.

You and your spouse are in the kitchen. The kids are in the family room playing checkers. Lower your voice so it's even harder for them to hear, and then comment, "Look at them concentrate. Sometimes I think there's not a single thing they can't accomplish if they put their minds to it."

Help Your Child Discover How He/She Learns Best

George sat next to me in several lectures while we attended the university. I liked to listen. Occasionally, I'd jot down a note or a major idea. While I was listening, George was feverishly writing down every word and phrase his hand could produce.

"George, did you hear that last point?" I'd occasionally ask.

"What point?"

"Did you understand what she just said about the maturation of thought processes from concrete to abstract?"

"Not a clue. Here, check my notes," George would say.

Later that day, George would review his notes. He'd try to make sense out of them and synthesize his learning by writing them out again in a slightly summarized version. By the time George had read his notes several times and written them in two or three versions, he fully understood the material.

George was very smart, and I respected his intelligence, but I failed to understand why he used such an inefficient method for learning. Years later, I began to understand how differently people learn. Then I respected George even more for the effort he put forward to ensure that he could learn in a lecture, when listening was clearly not his preferred learning mode. George was in his best attentional state when he was moving. His brain was alert and active when his body could move. When he was forced to sit, his attention waned, so he wiggled and fidgeted or wrote notes like a mad dog to keep his brain awake.

Studies suggest that only about 19 percent of adults are in their preferred learning and attentional mode when listening. About 35 percent learn best in the kinesthetic state (movement), and 46 percent prefer to learn in the visual mode. These reflect the activity-states that help you stay alert and mentally focused.

Many of you reading this book today are using different techniques to help you think and learn. Some find a comfortable armchair and relax while reading. Some read aloud, and others read the words silently. Some readers sip on drinks and munch snacks while they concentrate. Others take movement breaks every ten or fifteen minutes.

There are so many individual ways to think and learn. Howard Gardner wrote a book called *Frames of Mind* (Basic Books, 1983) that disputes the idea that intelligence reflects only verbal and analytical thinking. He described seven different ways of being smart and has recently added an eighth.

1. Linguistic: The intelligence of words.
2. Logical-Mathematical: The intelligence of reasoning.
3. Spatial: The intelligence of pictures and images.
4. Body-Kinesthetic: The intelligence of physical skill.
5. Musical: The intelligence of sound, rhythm, tone, and melody.
6. Interpersonal: The intelligence of getting along with others.
7. Intrapersonal: The intelligence of knowing yourself.
8. Naturalist: The intelligence of knowing and observing the rhythms, patterns, and details of nature.

Every child has abilities in each area, the potential to develop new skills in each type of intelligence, and a special preference for one or more of the types of intelligence. In school, there tends to be an emphasis on two kinds of intelligence. Can you guess which two? In schools where linguistic and logical-mathematical intelligence are overused, many children can't use their strengths and may get left behind. Some schools have begun to organize instruction around the idea that all children should have a chance to use their special strengths for at least a portion of every day. The Key School in Indianapolis, Indiana, is one example.

Still, there are more ways to understand the differences in learning style among children and among adults. Some people think in a step-by-step, sequential pattern, while others gather information in a random pattern from a variety of sources to form their thoughts, beliefs, and conclusions. Some people prefer to operate on the level of concrete thought, looking for practical application of ideas. Others enjoy thinking for the sake of thinking, and for them, the beauty of thought need not be sullied by practical application.

Some people prefer learning in the early morning, while some enjoy the late night. Some like bright lights, and others prefer dim. Some prefer to learn with lots of people around, and others learn best alone. Some people like to be told what to study, while others can't tolerate such an approach.

Do you see where this is leading?

Every child with attention problems (and every child without attention problems) is growing up in a world where lifelong learning is now required. Most of our children will change jobs and need to learn new skills several times during their working careers. Graduation from high school or college no longer means you can find a good job.

Using the skills of Love and Logic you can help your child learn to take responsibility for his own learning. Teaching him to recognize how he learns best will help him develop the skills to be an effective learner throughout life. In the appendix, you will find a booklet called "How I Learn Best," which is intended to help people recognize how they think, learn, organize, and perceive. With the help of an adult, any person twelve or older can begin to recognize individual strengths, effective learning strategies, and daily habits that will help him become an effective lifelong learner by using this material.

Purpose, Meaning, and Motivation

In his classic work, *Man's Search for Meaning* (Pocket Books/Simon and Schuster, 1980), Victor Frankl describes the horrors that men and women can endure if they live with a purpose. During Frankl's years in German concentration camps during World War II, he saw prisoners who ran to the wire and others who continued to live with inner dignity. "The prisoner who had lost faith in the future—his future—was doomed. With his loss of belief in the future, he also lost his spiritual hold; he let himself decline and become subject to mental and physical decay."

In Friedrich Nietzsche's words, "He who has a why to live for can bear with almost any how."

When you have purpose in your life, hope can live even in the most difficult situations. Frankl wrote about himself:

Another time we were at work in a trench. The dawn was gray around us; gray was the sky above; gray the snow in the pale light of dawn; gray the rags in which my fellow prisoners were clad; and gray their faces. I was again conversing silently with my wife, or perhaps I was struggling to find the reason for my suffering, my slow dying. In a last violent protest against the hopelessness of imminent death, I sensed my spirit piercing through the enveloping gloom. I felt it transcend that hopeless, meaningless world, and from somewhere I heard a victorious "Yes" in answer to my question of the existence of an ultimate purpose. At that moment, a light was lit in a distant farmhouse, which stood on the horizon as if painted there, in the midst of the miserable gray of a dawning morning in Bavaria. Et lux in tenebris lucet—and the light shineth in the darkness. For hours I stood hacking at the icy ground. The guard passed by, insulting me, and once again I communed with my beloved. More and more I felt that she was present, that she was with me; I had the feeling that I was able to touch her, able to stretch out my hand and grasp hers. The feeling was very strong: she was there. Then at that very moment, a bird flew down silently and perched just in front of me, on the heap of soil which I had dug up from the ditch, and looked steadily at me.

What does this mean for your child?

John and his mother sat in my office recently. He was big and strong, articulate and bright. He wasn't passing any classes, and his mother wanted me to determine what was wrong with him. Some learning problem, she surmised, was causing him to avoid all homework and pay little attention in class.

"I haven't done one piece of homework in three years," he told me candidly.

He looked at his mom. "I don't care if I pass these courses or if I ever graduate. It's just not my thing!"

"What do you care about?" I asked. "What's important to you?"

He looked at me with a little grin on his face. "Can't tell you that," he replied.

John's parents want him to do well in school. His father has offered him a brand new car if he'll just improve his schoolwork. That breaks my heart. John has traveled the world with his parents. He's bright and incredibly capable, but he's empty inside. He sees no "why" in his life.

Not Michael. This boy has some real problems. Michael's wiring has never been normal. Learning has never come easily. It took more than a year before he stopped getting lost in a small middle school. His sequential memory is poor and his organizational skills are troublesome.

Every night he goes through a routine he has posted above his desk to keep himself organized. He's passing all his classes. Last year he won a creative writing contest. Thank God for spell-check!

His single mom prayed and cried and hoped for years that he could learn to have a decent life, and he will. Everyday he helps with family chores. He lives with purpose and responsibility. He has a "why" in his life.

A spiritual life, chores, a family that holds you lovingly to high standards, more chores for the family, a sense of purpose, a belief that the people around you care about you deeply, the belief that you are competent to succeed, and the realization that through effort you can generally cause good things to occur in your life all lay the foundation for a meaningful existence.

An intention deficit will cripple a child more than any attention problem. May your children and all the children you know find purpose, giving them the fuel for great effort and lives filled with joy.

Relaxation Techniques

Christopher is a successful emergency room physician. His life is a blur of movement, action, and stimulation. During the quiet times at work, he jokes and plays pranks. Away from work, he seeks stimulation as well, going to games, quick trips up north, out to a party. He laughs when friends tell him he's hyper. Everyday he runs three miles. It helps him settle himself and focus on the tasks ahead. Once in a while, life gets a little too overwhelming for him, and he quietly disappears for ten or fifteen minutes. He finds a quiet place, then he visualizes using a specific routine he learned and brings his internal tension down to the level he knows works best for him. Then he charges back into the active flow of his life.

It wasn't always so. Christopher was a mediocre student in high school. He was the class clown, often disorganized and underprepared. School made him fidgety. Sometimes his smart mouth got him into trouble.

Even then, when life seemed overwhelming or a little out of control, Christopher had ways to relax. He began to drink a lot during his sophomore year, and then he dabbled in other drugs. He was seventeen when he went into rehab—when drug rehab programs were still available and covered by insurance. It was a four-week program, and one of the important lessons he learned was to take responsibility for his energy, state of mind, even his impulsivity. One of his counselors took a special interest in Christopher and helped him begin a path of learning how to achieve the mental, emotional, physical, and spiritual states that would help him become happy and productive.

For Christopher this meant running, controlling his internal dialogue, healthy relationships, avoiding drugs, and regular visualization. Each of these things took a little learning and a lot of practice. Christopher developed a lifestyle that allowed him to stay in a generally focused and positive mental state.

For your child, the relaxation techniques of choice might be different. Aerobic exercise, martial arts, hathayoga, helping an elderly neighbor, or long walks in a beautiful natural setting help some people manage tension and stress. In recent years, biofeedback training has helped many people with attention problems learn to reduce tension and improve attentional states. Progressive and autogenic relaxation techniques are included in most sophisticated athletic training programs and have been demonstrated to be an effective treatment for hyperactivity.

Children and adults with attention problems can develop strategies to help them deal with stressful events or periods in their life. Physical activity, relaxation, or biofeedback training will work for some. Others may be attracted to meditation, prayer, painting, working with wood, listening to music, dancing, or spending time with their siblings.

Christopher was lucky. He started down a path filled with heartache, but found the help and resources he needed to change his path. He learned some strategies that are healthier than what he had been doing and enable him to live a meaningful life. His life is active. He still craves stimulation and is occasionally impulsive, but he's a fine man and an outstanding physician.

Consider Family Therapy

Brad and Karen sat down at the front table in the library where the Love and Logic workshop was about to begin. They looked angry. They were seated in chairs next to each other, but they were not together. They pointed their chairs in different directions so they would not have to look at each other. Then Brad pulled his chair back against a shelf of books and crossed his arms over his chest.

As the workshop began, I noticed their pattern of interaction. When an example of helicopter parenting was introduced, Karen glared at her husband then looked away with disgust. When a story about drill sergeant parents was told, Brad poked his wife on the arm. "Are you listening to this? Are you listening?" he demanded.

Their nasty looks continued. As I was telling a story about logical consequences, Karen suddenly interrupted. "But what if you don't have any backup at home? What if your partner never backs you up?"

The other parents sitting with Karen and Brad were looking uncomfortable and tried not to notice their angry gestures as the evening workshop continued.

On the following Wednesday evening, the workshop reconvened and they were back, sitting in exactly the same chairs. This time only one woman was sitting with them at their table, and she had missed the first session. She wasn't aware of how they had behaved during the first week's session.

But something was different. They sat closer to each other. There were fewer angry looks. After the session was over, they stayed and talked with me for more than an hour. Their four children were a handful. Brad worked long hours. Their oldest son was ten years old and angry and mostly out of control. We brainstormed a plan for them to try during the next week.

On the following Wednesday evening, they came into the room and sat down at their usual place. Karen's face wasn't angry, and Brad sat close enough to his wife that their legs were slightly touching, even though there was plenty of room at their table.

"It's been a good week," they explained.

This was the last session of a three-evening workshop. Afterward, they lingered again and we talked.

Like so many people today, their lives are busy. Two of their four children have attention problems at school. Even with Karen devoting her time to staying home with the kids, the demands of family are overwhelming at times. They have no network of support to help them. No grandparents, aunts, uncles, or close neighbors to straighten them out from time-to-time. They feel they're trying to figure it out on their own. They need a little help.

Love and Logic can serve as a wonderful vehicle to encourage friendly discussion about parenting styles and child-rearing needs, but sometimes families need more. Like many couples, Karen and Brad slipped into an unhappy pattern. As Karen ordered, Brad hovered and protected. Seeing this, and not wanting her kids to be overprotected wimps, she became even more directive. Their parenting styles became more and more different and less compatible. Anger and anxiety increased in their home.

With easy, compliant children, parenting style differences or a lack of communication may not have brought on a family crisis. But some kids are tougher to raise than others. These children challenge parents to develop superior parenting skills, communication skills, empathy, organization skills, and a commitment to nurture one another.

At times, a child being diagnosed as having a disorder provides an easy way for a family to avoid facing serious family or personal issues. Johnny, the child with a disorder, becomes the focus of family concern and an easy explanation for the discord and tension within his family. However, it may not be all Johnny's doing.

Karen and Brad need a little help as they learn to work together to raise their beautiful children. Their family therapist was unfamiliar with Love and Logic but loved the concepts and wanted to learn. She's helping them stay focused on their goal to regain a calm, loving, respectful atmosphere at home. They're working to develop trust and effective communication between the two of them and to set limits for their children without becoming angry or emotionally destructive.

Sometimes families need help. Ask your minister or school counselor for a list of recommended family therapists, clarify what you hope therapy will accomplish, and be willing to interview a few therapists to see who's a good match for you.

Television, Videos, and Computer Games

One hundred and fifty channels, all the Disney videos, and fantastically creative nonviolent computer learning games offer children an incredible selection of stimulating video activities to keep them from ever getting bored. How sad.

What a poor substitute video magic can be for conversation at dinner, stories by the fireplace with Grandpa, running like young colts outdoors, learning to cook, playing catch, organizing a neighborhood game, putting on a circus, playing checkers or chess, working in the garden, kicking the soccer ball, playing imaginative games, digging holes in the backyard, drawing pictures, looking at clouds, reading books, or doing chores.

Video time does not teach interactive language, or teach you to persist or build attentional skills. In fact, the passive and repetitious nature of the experience may contribute mightily to habits of poor attention. Studies have demonstrated patterns of slower brainwave activity among children who watch too much TV or too many videos.

There are some who argue that the content of TV shows and video and/or computer games is often violent, sarcastic, disrespectful, and inappropriately sexual. Perhaps so. I argue that even if you carefully control the content of video exposure, anything more than five hours per week for a developing (under eight years) child is probably too much. One of the worst things you can do for a child with attention problems is lull him into complacency with video magic.

If Thomas Alva Edison had had a bedroom with his own TV, Nintendo, and computer games, would he have dreamed, wondered, built, and created? If Ben Franklin had been surrounded by video entertainment, would he have read great books, pondered the habits of nature, and imagined wonderful stories?

In childhood, the neural networks related to the activities you pursue are what develop. You grow what you use. Kids need to grow balance skills, agility, large muscle skills, listening skills, imagination, gumption, fine-motor skills, conversation, more listening skills, social skills, problem-solving skills, love of nature, the ability to use hands and eyes together, visualize, and remember visual images. For the most part, video magic gets in the way of developing these skills.

Music and Sound

Even in the womb, your child is hearing. The auditory cortex is developing with this experience. By the sixth month of uterine development, a baby can clearly distinguish her mother's voice, and will have a preference for this voice in the months after birth.

In the first year after birth, a rich auditory environment includes voices, rhythm, song, and instrumental music. The individual sounds of language begin to be discriminated and lay the foundation for language that the child will later produce. She is beginning to understand the incredibly complex patterns of sound that form language, including melody, meter, inflection, and the relationship to nonverbal cues. The patterns of symbolic language then become the foundation for the complex thinking skills that make humans unique.

So much of language and thinking skills depends on our ability to decipher the patterns of vibrational frequency that exist in the world round us. So much of our brainpower is devoted to the discrimination and understanding of sound.

The early years of language development are enhanced by good nutrition, good hearing, the development of balance and spatial aware-ness, interactive language with caregivers, emotional security, and the rich and beautiful patterns of sound called music. Children learn to recognize and understand increasingly complex sound patterns if they have the opportunity.

Some kids are not so lucky. Injury, infection, allergy, poor nutrition, or trauma may affect development. Or they may live in an environment without interactive language or beautiful music. Or they may be sur-rounded by harsh noise and never hear the beautiful melodies of nature.

The work of Tomatis, Berard, Campbell, and others makes it clear to me that we are just beginning to understand the uses of sound for healing and to support brain function and neurological development. We do know that music can be used to help some people improve their ability to sustain attention.

Many people need to calm themselves in order to find a relaxed state that allows sustained attention. Relaxing music helps them slow down inside and find their focus. For many people (including children) with attention problems this method won't work at all. Dr. Richard Lugar and others have shown that many people with attention problems have difficulty sustaining the patterns of high-frequency brainwaves we associate with the alertness required for symbolic thought, analysis, or problem solving. These folks are struggling to maintain alertness, and new age relaxation music might help them go to sleep but would make it even harder for them to remain alert. Music with a quick, steady beat, or complex patterns of high-frequency sound might help them stay better focused.

For some that means Mozart, Vivaldi, Pachelbel, Grieg, or Gregorian chant. For others it means easy listening background music. For still others it might even mean rock and roll pounding in the background to help them stay alert.

Please don't leap to the conclusion that all kids with attention problems need rock and roll or any other kind of music to help them concentrate. Each person responds differently. Try to be open and evaluate what works best for you or your child.

The Monroe Institute in Faber, Virginia, has pioneered research on the use of binaural beats to facilitate the achievement of specific brainwave states. They have found that by delivering slightly different tones to each side of the brain, it is possible to induce the brain into patterns of faster or slower brainwave activity. These patterns of sound can be put behind recorded music and used to either relax or enhance states of attention.

The development of wonderful listening skills enhances the development of analytic thinking, pattern recognition, and problem-solving skills. Music can help in the development of early listening skills, and music can be used to help sustain attention.

Music Training

In recent years the popular press has reported research that suggests early music training helps improve mathematical thinking. Indeed, it seems to be true. Researchers at the University of California, Irvine, studied preschoolers who took piano lessons and sang daily in a chorus and compared them with preschoolers who did not. After eight months, the musical preschoolers scored 80 percent higher than their peers on tests of spatial intelligence. These students could visualize shapes and patterns and understand how things fit together—qualities that enhance mathematical understanding. **Encourage your school board to fund music training**

The motor training involved in learning to play an instrument seems to be an important component of this early learning. In follow-up studies it was found that students who took only singing lessons did not make the same gains as their instrument-trained peers.

Many cultures and civilizations have recognized the value of musical training. For me to be a believer, it's enough to simply observe a young child playing a Mozart sonata and watching the calm concentration amidst the intricate finger work. Musical training supports memory training, recognition of patterns, sound discrimination, focused alertness, perseverance, and the appreciation of beauty. For many children, it offers an opportunity to excel.

Language, Thinking Skills, and Modeling

Billy and his dad headed out to the garage. "I wonder what tools we're going to need to build this doghouse?" asked his dad.

Together they speculated on the needed tools.

"Think we ought to build it here or in the backyard?"

They discussed the need to carry tools and the available electricity for the circular saw. They decided to build in the garage.

"Should we move out the cars from the garage or just work around them?"

They decided to move out one car.

"Do you think we need to draw out a plan or just wing it?"

There was a time when parents and children had to work together often for family survival. With improvements in our income levels, the disposable nature of many of our purchases, busy lifestyles, and fabulous entertainment systems, parents don't always have the same opportunities to model language, thinking, and organizational skills.

Planning for a building project or a cooking project provides a chance to help kids practice looking ahead. What tools will we need? Should we read the directions or just start mixing?

Walking to the window, one mother looks outside and wonders aloud, "Wonder how cold it is today. Perhaps I'd better take my gloves and boots. Looks like snow." She's modeling decision making based on looking ahead.

Most thinking skills don't just happen by mistake. Organizing a project, planning to stick with a task, even if things get tough, thinking about the welfare of another family member or a neighbor, showing respect for an elder or a younger; all these can be learned from modeling.

• • • • •

"Let's plan our menus for the week, and then we'll go shopping," said one parent.

• • • • •

"Let's design a place for bookbags and briefcases so we'll all know where to find our important papers in the morning," said another.

• • • • •

"What time do you think will work best as your regular study time?" asked one mom.

"I don't know."

"Do you think before dinner or after dinner would work better?"

"Probably after, because I'm hungry after school, then I like to play."

"We're usually done with dinner by 7:00 P.M. Then there's cleanup. How does 7:30 to 8:30 P.M. sound to you?"

• • • • •

"What do you think Mrs. Wilson is doing tonight?"

"Probably just watching *Jeopardy*."

"Let's surprise her with a nice dessert. What shall we make?"

• • • • •

"Wow, I had a rough day at work."

"Why don't you just quit? Those parent-teacher conferences sound so discouraging."

"It's hard work," said Mom sitting close to her daughter, "but it's not discouraging. Everyday I get to work with beautiful children. And some days, I get to help parents find ways to make their families stronger. When I think about it, I'm pretty blessed to be able to do my work."

"Mom, do you think I'll ever find a job I love that much?"

• • • • •

"Dad, did you remember we planned to go to the hands-on museum tomorrow?"

"Oh, no. I forgot."

"But, Dad."

"One of the guys at work has an extra ticket for the U of M game, and offered it to me."

"I guess we can go to the museum some other weekend."

"Thanks, buddy, but that's not a good plan for me. I've been needing to spend some time just with you."

"You sure?"

"Yep. I'll call Fred. There are lots of other people at work who would love to go to that game."

• • • • •

Our children learn vocabulary from interactive models. That means people, not TV. They learn thinking skills from observing you think, from your actions and your words. They develop skills of planning, organization, persistence, and delayed gratification by watching you and listening to you.

Of course, this takes time. Not the mystical "quality time" some experts talk about, just time.

chapter nine

Why Everything in This Book Applies to All Kids, Not Just Those with Attention Problems

All children need parents who provide consequences, empathy, love, humor, and a sense of faith.

The tools and techniques of parenting children are largely the same whether or not the child has a learning problem, A.D.H.D., a physical handicap, or some other condition.

Great parents are great parents, no matter what the child's problem. We learned that in working with our foster parents over the years. We worked with many children who had a variety of psychological, social, and neurological disorders. No matter what the child's problems, the parents who were most successful used the same skills, basic foundation tools, and techniques. They all used Love and Logic techniques!

We did a very thorough study trying to ascertain the foundational characteristics of great parents. And in addition to the child management and discipline techniques, we found two variables that all effective parents seemed to have in common:

A sense of humor
A sense of faith

These are actually personality attributes that can be practiced and developed. They are attitudes that, in addition to the Love and Logic tools that our professional parents had been taught, seemed to help them be effective with very difficult children.

A sense of humor allows parents to step back, keep things in perspective, and laugh when others might be wringing their hands with concern. One parent laughingly said, "I've worked years trying to catch Robert doing the right thing at the right time in the right way. But I've pretty much decided that two out of three is good enough!

A sense of faith allows parents to know they cannot control all situations all the time. The faith-filled parents know that many things are between their child and God. One mom said, "Sometimes I think it would take a miracle for Jeff to be able to handle the other children without going off the deep end. I've talked to him on many occasions, but I'm very poor at miracles. God is very good at miracles. So I blow some things off to him, and I always think God is pretty appreciative, 'Oh, good, Nancy doesn't think she can handle all problems, all the time, and leaves some to me.' Maybe God likes that kind of humility."

It is easy to see why the right attitudes are so effective, but why are the Love and Logic techniques so universally effective?

All children need choices and consequences for thoughtless and impulsive behavior.

Love and Logic makes several assumptions that are almost always true for all children—except in the cases of very disturbed children. Love and Logic assumes:

The child can learn from bad and good experiences.
The child is capable of feeling an attachment or love for adults— and there is at least some desire to please.

These two personality aspects are present in almost all children, regardless of whether they learn fast or slow; are compliant or oppositional. Let's look at how Love and Logic consequences were applied with a very difficult oppositional child:

Ty was a very disturbed seven-year-old. In fact, when he was to be picked up at the airport, I had been concerned how safe the foster mother, Doris, might be on her hour and a half drive from the Denver airport to her ranch home in Elizabeth, Colorado.

"Oh, don't you never mind about me, Foster," she said, "I'm taking James in the station wagon with me." Well, James was a very troublesome and two-thirds ferocious thirteen-year-old with impulse problems of his own, so I knew he would help Doris out.

When I talked to Doris the following week and asked her how it had gone on her trip to the airport to pick up Ty, she replied, "Lord-a-mercy, Foster, James was beggin' for mercy himself before we ever cleared Denver!" Then she went on to tell me that Ty had broken the back window of her vehicle.

Well, Ty had been a real fighter, and when he came up to the clinic several weeks later, I asked him how his fighting was going. He answered, saying, "I'm not fighting much anymore."

"Really!" I replied, somewhat surprised. Then I kidded, "Why not, Ty? How could you give that up? You were best at fighting other kids. Fighting was your forte."

"I hate doing all the chores!"

When he said, "I hate doing all the chores," I must have looked a little puzzled, as I didn't see how doing chores fit sensibly as a logical consequence for fighting. But then again, hey, whatever works!

Ty explained to me, "My mom says that when I fight with other kids, it drains her energy! But when I clean behind the refrigerator with a brush, she says it puts energy back into her, and *I hate putting energy into my mom!*"

Let's look at the great Love and Logic principles that this mom was using:

- She put herself first, saying what *she was feeling or thinking*, not what the child was doing wrong. In fact, I'm sure that if she said, "Ty, quit hitting Kirk," he would have hit Kirk harder and faster. But she was more effective talking about herself, "Ty, honey, I feel an energy drain coming on." Boy did that put the brakes on the kid in a hurry!

- She gave choices implicitly: The behavior could continue, and Ty could make up the energy drain. The choice was his. She didn't say "stop it."

- She used consequences with empathy to help Ty learn from his mistakes: "It must be miserable spending hours behind the refrigerator cleaning the linoleum. What a bummer!" But she also gave encouragement: "If anyone can make a big beautiful difference in how things look (back there where no one will ever see it), it's you!"

- She was respectful but firm. Caring and loving without being a pushover. And she was consistent.

So, as difficult as Ty might be, he had two wonderful qualities necessary to grow to be a great Love and Logic human being: He had the capacity for love, and he had causal thinking. So consequences and love were effective.

When Jim Fay and I do workshops across America, we often run into parents who spontaneously say, "You know, I've used those techniques with my A.D.H.D. child. I didn't think they would work. But they work like magic."

All children need encouragement.

When using the Love and Logic techniques, special children do require lots of support and encouragement. They need lots of statements like:

"Boy, I bet you feel good about that!"
"You remembered that all on your own, didn't you?"
"Wow! Two gold stars today! What will you bring home next?"

It is *very* easy for tired parents—and A.D.H.D. kids are tiring—to focus on what the child does *wrong* and give their emotion to that. But when the child does things impulsively, incorrectly, or thoughtlessly, wise Love and Logic parents are mostly low key and help the child accept the consequences of their behavior or quietly start the problem solving: "What do you think you need to do with Joyce to make things right, now that her favorite doll is headless?"

It is so easy to explode when things go wrong! "What have you done!!! You tore Samantha's head right off!!! You're going to have to pay for this and apologize to Joyce!"

Love and Logic parents practice being noisy about good behavior and quiet about poor behavior.

All children misbehave more when parents show frustration.

Raising children can at times be frustrating. And our special children may give us more to feel frustrated about. No one can run a business, participate in a marriage, or raise children without times of frustration. *And although everyone feels frustration, the great leaders and great parents show it less!* It's true! Think of the people you know and respect, and there is every chance that they manage to show minimal frustration. In fact, during the worst of times, one great president said encouragingly, "The only thing we have to fear is fear itself."

All children are unconsciously thrilled when their parents show frustration. And such parents can easily turn a mistake or thoughtless action by their child into a habit. All children thrive on frustration for two reasons.

When parents show frustration, they give the child one thing no child can refuse: emotion.

Emotion keeps the spinal cord from shriveling! We pay any individual who gives us emotion big bucks. Whether it is a movie star in Hollywood or a football or baseball player in the field. We seldom pay people big bucks for doing good. We generally pay folks big bucks to give us emotion. So children will do anything to get their parents to emote. Making a mother light up, turn red, and go off is a lot more fun than a Fourth of July sparkler.

Many a livid mother has come into my office, fairly shouting, "He knows what upsets me! He knows how to push my buttons! He does this because he knows I really abhor it!"

In situations like this, I always think to myself, "Golly, I've only been watching this little show for about fifteen seconds, but it is good!!" And a tiny horrible little boy voice, even in me, says, "It sure would be fun to be her kid!"

When parents show frustration they give the child control. After all, almost all parents who show frustration are saying pretty clearly that *they*, the parent, don't have control. A kid doesn't have to be a wizard in interpersonal relations to know that if the parent doesn't have control, then *he or she must have it!*

Great parents of frustrating kids get very good at venting on their spouse when their child isn't around. Or they wait to vent their feelings in a Love and Logic class. Or best of all, when they are frustrated and don't know what to say, they *shut up!*

Rather than lose control, it is far better to say to a child, "Honey, I have good news and I have bad news. The good news for you is that right now I'm feeling frustrated and I don't know what to say, so I'm not going to say anything! The bad news for you is that we will talk at 3:00 tomorrow afternoon."

Of course the child is usually a little nonplused, wondering what the parent is going to say. As most great parents walk off, they wonder what they are going to say, too. But at least they have a day to figure it out!

Remember, telling a child you are frustrated or angry or upset—as long as you have good self-control—is far different than fruitlessly and ineffectively *showing* those feelings. The first is called talking it out— which is healthy; and the second is called acting it out—which is tacky!

Are A.D.H.D. kids often trying? You bet! Can they wear you out? Absolutely! What works? A lot of the same things that work for all kids. And the great foster parents that I have known over the years do well with both A.D.H.D. and non-A.D.H.D. kids. They do well with behaviorally disturbed kids and do well with "near normal" kids. Why? Because they are Love and Logic parents. They are slow in showing frustration and they avoid control battles. They give choices and consequences with empathy. They model talking about feelings and not exploding them out.

References

Bellak, L., and Black, R.B. Attention deficit hyperactivity disorder in adults, *Clin. Ther.* 14 (1992): 138–147.

Biederman J., Baldessarini, R. J., Wright, V., Knee, D., Harmatz, J.S., and Goldblatt, A. A double-blind placebo controlled study of desipramine in the treatment of ADD: II. Serum drug levels and cardiovascular findings, *J. Am. Acad. Child Adolesc. Psychiatry* 28 (1989): 903–911.

Faraone, S.V., Biederman, J., Keenan, K., and Tsuang, M.T. A family-genetic study of girls with DSM-III attention deficit disorder, *Am. J. Psychiatry* 148 (1991): 112–117.

Greenfield, B., Hechtman, L., and Weiss, S. Two subgroups of hyperactives as adults, *Can. J. Psychiatry* 33 (1988): 505–508.

Klein, R.G. Prognosis of attention deficit disorder and its management in adolescence, *Pediatr. Rev.* 8 (1987): 216–222.

Liu, C., Robin, A.L., Brenner, S., and Eastman, J. Social acceptability of methylphenidate and behavior modification for treating attention deficit hyperactivity disorder, *Pediatrics* 88 (1991): 560–565.

McGee, R., Partridge, F., Williams, S., and Silva, P.A. A twelve-year follow-up of preschool hyperactive children, *J. Am. Acad. Child Adolesc. Psychiatry* 30 (1991): 224–232.

Offord, D.R., Boyle, M.H., Fleming, J.E., Blum, H.M., and Grant, N.I. Ontario Child Health Study: Summary of selected results, *Can. J. Psychiatry* 34 (1989): 483–491.

Ratey, J.J., Greenberg, M.S., and Lindem, K.J. Combination of treatments for attention deficit hyperactivity disorder in adults, *J. Nerv. Merit Dis.* 179 (1991): 699–701.

Rieder—Uysal, D. Are there sex differences in the manifestation of hyperkinetic syndrome? *Z. Kinder Jugenpsychiatr.* 18 (1990): 140–145.

Rostain, A.L. Attention deficit disorders in children and adolescents, *Pediatr. Clin. North Am.* 38 (1991): 607–635.

Shaywitz, S.E., and Shaywitz, B.A. Diagnosis and management of attention deficit disorder: A pediatric perspective, *Pediatr. Clin. North Am.* 31 (1984): 429–457.

Shekim, W.O., Asarnow, R.F., Hess, E.B., Zaucha, K., and Wheeler, N. A clinical and demographic profile of a sample of adults with attention deficit hyperactivity disorder, residual state, *Compr. Psychiatry* 31 (1990): 416–425.

Shekim, W.O., Masterson, A., Cantwell, D.P., Hanna, G.L., and McCracken, J.T. Nomifensine maleate in adult attention deficit disorder, *J. Nerv. Merit Dis.* 177 (1989): 296–299.

Weiss, G., and Hechtman, L. *Hyperactive Children Grown Up.* New York: Guilford Press, 1986.

Wender, P.H., and Reimherr, F.W. Bupropion treatment of attention-deficit hyperactivity disorder in adults, *Am. J. Psychiatry* 147 (1990): 1018–1020.

Woolf, A.D., and Zuckerman, B.S. Adolescence and its discontents: Attentional disorders among teenagers and young adults, *Pediatrician* 13 (1986): 119–127.

Zametkin, A. J., and Borcherding, B.G. The neuropharmacology of attention deficit hyperactivity disorder, *Annu. Rev. Med.* 40 (1989): 447–451.

Zametkin, A. J., Nordahl, T.E., Gross, M., et al. Cerebral glucose metabolism in adults with hyperactivity of childhood onset, *N. Engl. J. Med.* 323 (1990): 1361–1366.

chapter ten

The Home Program

Parents have used the steps of the home program for children with attentional challenges or challenging behaviors. This program lays the foundation for school success and increases the odds that your child will spend some valuable time wondering, "How's my next decision going to affect me?"

The steps in this process are sequential. Each new phase is dependent on the previous step being established. Generally, you'll find that progress gets easier as you build confidence and your child comes to believe you can handle the challenges he presents.

The Home Program helps your child learn to see his parents as firm, loving, authority figures. It also helps him realize that mistakes are human, you'll always love him, people learn from mistakes, and there are usually consequences to poor decisions.

Think of this chapter as a basic outline that you can use to help you chart your course. By developing a few good ideas that might work for you at each step of the Home Program, you'll have a repertoire of responses for the challenges to come. Focus on one issue at a time. Only when you're confident that each step is firmly established in the home should you move on to the next step.

The Home Program

1. Neutralize arguments
2. Learn to use enforceable statements
3. Never break a sweat
4. Establish a routine for the first hour of the morning
5. Establish a working relationship with your child's teacher(s)
6. Develop a recovery time routine
7. Food issues
8. Chores
9. Only good minutes are spent in the classroom
10. Homework

   Jim Fay and Bob Sornson

Neutralize Arguments

Smart, manipulative, and challenging youngsters of any age are masters at the game of sucking us into no-win arguments and rationalizations.

"You are three hours late," an angry parent stated the obvious.

"So what?"

"Do you know how much your mother and I have been worrying?"

"She's not my real mother. Besides, what do you care? Since you married her, she's the only one who counts."

"How can you say that?" his father replies sincerely. (The focus on the problem is already lost.) "You know how much we love you. Both of us. How can you not realize…"

Love and Logic parents try to avoid being sucked into brain-draining arguments and explanations.

Doing it right

"Thank God you're all right. I was really worried about you," the Love and Logic parent might proclaim.

"So what if I'm late?" the rebelling teen replied.

"I'm too emotionally exhausted to explain, and I sure don't want to argue. Try not to worry about it. We can talk about it in the morning."

· · · · ·

Alexandra loves her television shows, even though the rule of the house is no more than one half-hour show per day. When Mom turns it off, she begins:

"Not fair. *Barney*'s coming on. I love *Barney*."

"I know," says her mom.

"Can't I just watch a little?"

"Sorry, sweetie. What's the rule?"

"I hate the rule. Mary's house doesn't have a stupid rule like that."

"I know."

"Could you just let me watch this once?"

"What's the rule?"

"Sometimes Dad lets me watch two shows."

"Oh, that is sad. And what's the rule?"

Alexandra may be persistent, but she's no match for a mother who goes brain-dead and refuses to get sucked into the argument.

· · · · ·

Colin just decided he doesn't like peas. It's a silly thing to argue about, but some kids just like to test the waters.

"You're making peas? You know I can't stand peas."

"Really?"

"They make me sick!"

"That's so sad."

"They make me throw-up."

"Bummer."

"You can't make peas for dinner. Put them away."

"Really? Colin, are you planning to use nice words at dinner tonight, or are you thinking you just might skip a meal?" (Without sarcasm.)

"I'll use nice words. But if you loved me you wouldn't make peas."

"Nice try, Colin."

• • • • •

Dan is a teenager and has been testing some more serious waters.

"Dad, I need the car tonight. The coach asked us to go to his house for pizza."

"Oh, boy. That makes me sad. I guess I'm still worrying about your possible use of alcohol in my car."

"But, Dad, that was a month ago. And I only drank one beer."

"Probably so."

"How much longer are you going to worry about one stupid beer?"

"I don't know."

"Nobody else has a father like you."

"Probably."

"The coach is expecting me. And I told Brad I could pick him up."

"That's sad, Dan. I'll let you know when I've stopped worrying. Do you have any ideas for another ride to the coach's house?"

Parents can neutralize arguments by going brain-dead, not explaining, especially in the face of a control battle, and picking a few lines to use over and over. "I know," "Bummer," "It's so sad."

Learn to Use Enforceable Statements

"I'll be serving breakfast at 7:15 A.M. sharp."

"Are you going to pack your lunch or hire me to do it?"

"I'll be listening to you after your brother has finished talking to me."

"I listen to people who speak with a voice as soft as mine."

"Feel free to stay with us when you keep your hands to yourself."

"I drive kids to practice if they arrive home on time."

"Feel free to play with your friends when your chores are done."

"I'll be serving dessert to kids who eat a good dinner."

"I wash clothes that are put in the laundry room."

"Please join us for a game of checkers when your homework is done."

"Sure I'll help you with your homework. The first half hour is free."

"Those who follow the rules are welcome to play the game."

"Feel free to borrow the family car once I don't feel worried about the use of drugs or alcohol."

"Go to sleep this minute." (Just kidding.)

"Sweet dreams. I'll be serving breakfast at 7:15 A.M. sharp."

By using thinking words and enforceable statements, we set limits without telling our kids what to do this minute. They get to do some thinking while we set respectful boundaries for ourselves. We get to avoid the use of fighting words, which tend to cause control battles and resentment.

Some kids get angry and try to push your buttons when parents change their behavior.

"I hate it when you smile and give me choices."

"I know."

"I hate it when you say 'I know.'"

"That's sad."

"You and Mom just go around smiling and saying 'I know' or 'that's sad.' It makes me sick! I liked things better the old way. Before you went to that stupid Love and Logic class."

One little boy lived in a family where verbal and physical abuse was common until his parents studied Love and Logic.

"Are things better now?" he was asked.

"I suppose. My dad doesn't hit me so much, and my parents aren't yelling all the time."

"Is that better?"

"I guess. But now they just smile at me, and I don't get my way. I can't get away with anything without earning chores or something."

Children desire predictable behavior. Strangely, they may even desire unhealthy predictable behavior and have difficulty adapting to change. For a while, they may test your new parenting style until it gradually becomes predictable. It may even take a few months and then...

"Dad, can I borrow ten bucks? I really need it. I'm buying a new tire for my bike."

"Great. Is that the tire you broke doing jumps?"

"Yeah. Can I have the money? David's waiting."

"When do I give allowance?"

"Saturday. But I don't want to wait!"

"I know."

"Dad, I don't like waiting for things."

"Yeah. I know that feeling."

"Oh rats. I told David I wouldn't get an advance from you."

"You did? Why?"

"I just knew."

"Thanks for knowing, pal."

Never Break a Sweat

Some parents work so hard to be good parents. The kids know when we're struggling or unsure, in much the same way as a dog can sense fear.

"You're not going anywhere until your room is clean."

"But, Mom, the team needs me."

"Hurry up now. We have five more minutes. Look at all these clothes under your bed. Some of these are clean clothes. Oh, Danny. What's the matter with you? Now they all stink."

"I didn't know."

"Hurry up now. Put this away."

"Where does it go?"

"Fine," says Danny's mom in exasperation. "Get in the car. I'll clean this mess later. But things are going to change around here. You hear me?"

When children watch us rant, rave, and then rescue, they quickly learn that what we say and do are often not consistent. They learn how to control our facial expressions, tone of voice, and even the little reddish blotches on the side of our necks.

Opposition tendencies are encouraged by 3Rs (rant, rave, and rescue) and by any tendency toward inconsistency.

Establishing our firm, loving authority in the home means convincing our beautiful children that we can handle them without breaking a sweat. Watch Mom after practicing Love and Logic for a while.

More Examples:

"Oh Danny," Mom might announce early in the week, "I'll be taking kids to sports on Saturday if their rooms are in good shape."

"O.K., Mom."

"And Danny, is it fair for me to expect you to know what a clean room is like?"

"Yes, Mom. You've shown me."

And then she prays, not that he'll always remember to clean his room, but that he'll make enough great mistakes to learn to be a wonderful man.

"Mom, let's go. We're going to be late. Why didn't you tell me it was time for my game?"

As she enjoys her coffee, without rushing she explains, "I take kids to sports when their rooms are in good shape."

"No fair! We've gotta go. The team needs me."

"I know. And I take kids to sports when their rooms are in good shape."

· · · · ·

"I'm not going to time-out. I hate that thinking rug."

"Uh-oh," Mom sings. "Sounds like a bad decision. Would you like to go to the rug with your feet on the ground or your feet in the air?"

Smiling drives your kids crazy. It makes them think that you don't have a problem, but possibly they do have a problem.

"Don't worry, sweetheart," says Mom with a smile. "If you're too tired to do your chores, I'll do them for you."

"No, no," says Suzie. She remembers having to weed the garden to make up for the last time she forgot to complete her chores.

Some kids even like to push their parents's buttons. One fellow used to argue with his kids about their extravagant tastes and tendency to waste money. So they goaded him at every opportunity. Then he took a Love and Logic course.

"Dad, I need a new bike. My old one sucks!"

He smiled. (It helps some of us relax our breathing.) Then he said, "You should have a new one. You'd look great on a new bike. That old one of yours is at least six months old."

"I should?"

"Sure. There's a lot of great bikes out there."

"And you'll get one for me?"

"I don't recall saying that. But let me know when you have enough money saved. I'd like to go along and see what you pick out."

Love and Logic parents avoid arguments and control battles by using enforceable statements, thinking words, sincere questions, choices, and empathy. They smile at their kids a lot.

• • • • •

"Mom, I need fifty bucks," said one nineteen-year-old.

"Probably so," she replied.

"You've gotta give it to me."

"Some kids think that way," she replied.

"If you don't give me the money, I'm going to have to start selling drugs," he raised the ante.

"Bummer," she replied. "That would be so sad."

"What do you mean?"

His mom explained, "If any kid could handle selling drugs it would probably be you. But eventually you'd get caught or hurt, and that would be so sad."

"Aren't you going to stop me?"

"How can I stop you?" she asked sincerely. "You're nineteen. You're a man. You'd probably make enough money to hire a good lawyer. Besides, I bet there are some guys in prison just dying to have a cute new cellmate."

"Mom, I can't believe you. I just want some money."

"I know," she smiled. "Good luck earning it."

Establish a Routine for the First Hour of the Morning

Some children need no help getting organized. Even in a disorganized home environment, they plan ahead, check for homework assignments, pack a lunch, remember to get permission slips signed, know where to find their backpacks, and catch the bus!

Other kids need help. Most five-year-olds need help getting organized for school. Gradually children learn to plan ahead, refer to a written assignment planner, write important dates on a calendar, keep their important papers in a special place, and other organizational skills.

There are intrinsic and extrinsic reasons for variations in organizational skills. Some children seem genetically inclined to organize. Others live in homes where attention to organization is modeled and expected.

Jackie does not. As a third grader she is beginning to experience the organizational demands of life. Each day she is assigned about ten minutes of homework. Occasionally there are permission slips to be signed or schoolwork to bring home. Much of it gets lost.

By the time Jackie gets up in the morning, her mother is gone to work. Her dad is just getting to sleep from his night job. Sometimes Jackie's brother helps her get some breakfast, but more often, he's running late. Usually he just grabs a Mountain Dew and heads off to high school.

Getting up in the morning isn't hard for Jackie. She brushes her teeth, then usually turns on the TV downstairs, so it won't bother Dad. Occasionally, she loses track of time and misses the bus. Then she has to wake up her father to catch a ride. Usually she skips breakfast.

> **The Home Program for children with attentional challenges or challenging behaviors suggests that many kids need help learning and practicing good organizational skills. Remember, talking with your child about new skills or routines should happen when the parents and child are happy with each other, not during a moment of frustration.**

The goal for all children is that they learn to be responsible for themselves over time. All young children need help getting started with their day, and some children will continue to need support and structure for a little longer than others. Parents gradually withdraw support as they know their children are capable of handling their organizational needs.

No clear age guidelines will be given in this chapter, because many of you are beginning the process of using Love and Logic with children of varied ages and needs, and because the needs of your children are intrinsically different. Instead, we'll offer a general plan for the first hour of the day that can begin when your child is five or fifteen.

1. Pick one person who can consistently follow through with your child. If that's impossible, let one parent communicate with whomever is helping and supporting the process when you are not available.

2. Start the night before. Use ten minutes to discuss the day to come and be sure schoolwork is stored in one consistent place (shelf, bookbag, or backpack in the kitchen). Use this as a time for happy talk, not lingering over problems. For young children, help them pick out clothes for the next day.

3. Develop a consistent wake-up routine. Gradually move to an alarm clock routine so your child thinks it is her responsibility to get up on time.

4. Model organizational thinking. Open your briefcase and think out loud. "I wonder if I'm all prepared for tomorrow. Pen, notebook, organizer. Here's my report. Here's my list of customers. I think I'm ready."

   Help your child by modeling task completion, planning ahead, and putting first things first. "I'd really like to watch the basketball game, but tonight I promised to help Mom paint the guest room."

5. Model good eating habits. Choose good foods and create a happy atmosphere that supports good digestion and disposition.

6. Avoid TV in the morning routine. Instead, encourage conversation and togetherness.

7. If your children pack a lunch, help them while they're young. Offer choices. Gradually let them take over the job.

8. Keep backpacks or books in a special location so your child doesn't have to search at the last minute. You may want to check to be sure this is done before breakfast is served for some children. "Feel free to have breakfast when you have your backpack."

9. Let your child help you develop or revise your morning routine. In extreme cases it is helpful to write out the steps of your morning routine. For young children, you could make a series of drawings or photographs that demonstrate the morning routine.

10. Gradually withdraw yourself from responsibility for reviewing homework, waking up your child, checking the backpack, packing the lunch, and getting her out the door on time. Try to continue to practice happy meals and conversations about your upcoming day.

Establish a Working Relationship with Your Child's Teacher(s)

One fourth grade teacher wisely advises her new parents, "I'll promise to believe half of what I hear about you, if you promise to believe half of what you hear about me."

Without a good working relationship between parent and teacher, many children will take advantage of the situation to help create mistrust and animosity.

Some parents write a letter at the beginning of the school year describing the child's strengths and needs, explaining how they are using Love and Logic at home and asking for frequent feedback. Other parents request a meeting early in the year, or spend time in school as volunteers.

Relationship building is not phony. It's an attempt to know the people who will influence the life of your child.

Unfortunately there are parents today who ask the school to take too much responsibility for their child. By helping educators know you are not that kind of parent, you can easily build a bond. Teachers want to be successful. They want your child to grow, learn, and prosper.

If your child has significant attentional or behavioral problems, begin by agreeing that the first step is to get your child to be in class without disturbing the learning environment for others. Alternative settings for your child are carefully described in the next chapter. Under some circumstances, your child should not be in school and must come home.

As you establish the Home Program, you will have reasonable consequences if your child is sent home. These may include quiet time during school hours, chores to make up for any time or inconvenience to you, or the cost of hiring "Mabel" to supervise your child.

If getting your child to be in class without disturbing others is your present goal, don't worry right now about work completion. That comes later.

Explain to your child, "Some kids soak up knowledge like a sponge, even if they choose not to complete assignments. Maybe you'll be one of those. Won't it be interesting to find out?"

At the beginning of your Love and Logic Home Program, ask the teacher to sit with you and your child so that it's clear that the adults are on the same team.

"I want him to be in class listening and learning for every good minute possible," you might say.

"Perhaps if he's getting antsy, you could have him run an errand in the school for you. Good behavior in class is our first goal. We'll get to learning and completing assignments next."

"Some teachers have a quiet place in the back of the room for kids who are starting to feel overwhelmed. Do you have a place like that? Of course, I understand he could use that place only if he does not disturb others."

"Some teachers have a deal worked out with the teacher down the hall so a kid can sit somewhere else for a while without disturbing others. Is that a possibility?"

"Sometimes schools have a special room in which kids can recover their self-control and get ready to learn some more. No? That's sad."

"If you ever get to the point where my child is disrupting the learning environment for others in such a way that you can no longer handle him, please know that you should call us. We have a plan so that he can be supervised at home. It won't be a lot of fun for him."

"We also have a long-term plan that we're working on. With time we are sure he'll be ready to complete school assignments and homework assignments. He's smart, and he's a good boy. As soon as he's ready to begin to really show us what he can do in school, we'll get together again and coordinate our efforts. Thanks for helping him have as many good minutes in school as possible."

Develop a Recovery Time Routine

Developing parental control over recovery time is a necessary part of the Home Program. Unfortunately, more children who have never stayed in recovery time are coming to American schools. Kids who won't go to recovery time think they are in control of the home. How sad! And how frightening it must be for a four-year-old who realizes that her parents aren't even able to handle her. How could they ever keep her safe from the scary things that may exist in the world?

Establishing control over recovery time is easiest with young children.

"Uh-oh. Bad decision, Roger. Guess you need a little recovery time."

"Please, I'll be good."

"Probably, but now it's recovery time."

"Not fair!"

"Would you like to walk or be carried?"

"No, no, no!"

"I guess that means carried."

Please keep in mind that recovery time is not punishment. It's a logical consequence to the child's decision to act badly. The child gets to think.

The parents get to enjoy a few moments without annoying behavior.

Recovery time starts when the child is in the recovery-time spot (chair, stairs, rug, or room) and has stopped any yelling or tantrums. When he's quiet and thinking, you can reasonably call this "thinking time."

Some experts calculate specific amounts of time by age for recovery time. That's probably fine. We suggest that four or five minutes of thinking time is enough for most small children.

Occasionally, an exception to this rule is made for parents who need ten minutes to regain their composure before they can be ready to parent with love.

No lectures are delivered upon placing the child into time-out.

"Please, Roger. You know how Daddy loves you. We just want you to be a good boy. We only put you into your room because we can't let you climb the curtains any more. It's the fourth set of curtains you've destroyed."

Begging, lecturing, and threatening only encourage Roger to argue or resist. As you close the door, or walk away from the rug, just smile and think of the few delicious moments of quiet you will enjoy. Roger doesn't need explanations. He knows why he's there. Nor does he need a stopwatch.

"When can I come out?"

"We'll let you know. Try not to worry about it," reply Roger's parents.

After a few minutes, it's time to give Roger some control.

"Feel free to come back as soon as you're sweet and quiet."

Some kids will recover immediately. Others want a moment of control and will wait a few more minutes. Great! Give Roger his moment. When he comes back, simply welcome him without any reminders.

Most young children need a few experiences with recovery time. Children with challenging behaviors or attentional challenges may need a few more.

Every time you use recovery time with anger or lecture, you reduce the thinking and learning opportunity for your child. When the child spends time thinking about your anger, he does not think about his poor behavior. When the child feels his sense of dignity has been diminished by your lectures, he does not think about his poor choices.

Anger and lecture reduce thinking and learning.

Children with challenging behaviors or attentional challenges are likely to keep testing you if you use recovery time with anger or lecture. A firm, calm approach works best with all kids, and especially the hard to reach child.

As children get older, you may encounter some additional challenges with recovery time, especially if you are just beginning to establish firm, loving adult authority in the home.

The recovery time approach will only work if kids like to be around the adult in the home and if the recovery time spot is not a rewarding place to be. A bedroom used for recovery time does not have to be barren, but should not be an entertainment center. TV, computer, and other video entertainment systems should be removed from the bedroom if you expect it to serve as a thinking spot

Occasionally, children refuse to stay in recovery time. Carrying them back in once or twice will sometimes be enough. With some children, you may need to hold the door closed until quiet and thinking has begun. Once in a while, a child has been able to assert so much power around the home that he will not stay in his room without the door being locked from the outside. A parent should stay near the room and listen until his tantrum diminishes and he begins to calm down. If he destroys some toys, don't replace them. After he's calm, give him a few minutes for thinking, then invite him to come out when he's feeling sweet. *Resist the urge to lecture.*

If your child has made a mess out of his room, you may wish to help him clean up at a later hour, without lecture. Or you may let him live with the mess for a while. Or you may invite him to join you for his next meal once the room is put back into reasonable order.

• **Recovery time is for thinking, not punishment.**
• **Recovery time starts when it's quiet and thinking has begun.**
• **A few minutes of thinking are usually enough.**
• **Anger, lecture, and reminders don't help.**
• **Some kids need more experience with recovery time than others.**

When your child consistently goes to recovery time when asked and stays there without a tantrum, you are ready for the next step in the Home Plan.

Food Issues

The basic food groups for Jacob included macaroni and cheese, fruit loops, milk, apple juice, and frozen chicken nuggets. That's it. That's all he would eat.

Children who control what they eat, when they eat it, and whether they sit in front of the TV while eating have come to believe that they are in charge of the home. How sad!

Enforceable statements can be used to help establish who's in charge of food without using fighting words.

"Dinner will be on the table for thirty minutes. Try to get enough good food to get you to your next meal."

"Kids who eat a good dinner can have dessert."

"Feel free to stay at the table if you treat others with respect."

Sometimes choices can be offered.

"Would you like peas or corn tonight?"

"Do you prefer candlelight or the overhead light?"

"Would you like to enjoy dinner with us or eat alone in the laundry room?"

Too much control over food choices for young children can be harmful. Many children today expect to snack on sugary foods whenever they want. Some expect tasty bribes to elicit their occasional good behavior. Parents establish themselves as loving authority figures in the home by appropriately controlling food choices.

One wise mother designated a shelf in the refrigerator to "anytime" eating. The shelf was always well stocked with fruits and vegetables. She told her kids, "Anytime you are in need of a snack, eat all you want from that shelf. Food from the other shelves is off-limits."

If her kids ate from the other shelves without permission, she charged them market price plus a delivery charge (usually a $5 surcharge).

Chores

Once **Recovery Time** and control over **Food Issues** are established, you are ready for the magic of chores.

Many children today do not feel valuable to their families. They use family resources, but give very little back. Chores for the family give children a sense of importance, of being needed. Chores can give children a sense of accomplishment through struggle. Kids who do chores learn persistence.

In past years, families needed children to help with the vegetable garden, feeding animals, gathering eggs. Today, that's often not the case. Sometimes it's easier for parents to hire a job done or to just do it themselves. How sad. Kids that don't contribute to the family feel less bonded and less valued.

Brad helped make it clear. He was fifteen, strong, smart, well traveled, and well dressed. He was choosing to do nothing in school.

"Do you have any chores at home?"

"Sure. Sometimes I feed my goldfish. But usually not. I guess most of the time I let the maid feed them."

> **Our goal in the Home Program is to let each child who is**
> **eight years or older do fifteen to thirty minutes of chores for**
> **the family without being reminded every day.**

One way to instill a good attitude about work around the home is to model a good attitude. Whining about adult chores teaches children to avoid kid chores.

"I'm going to feel great when I get this lawn finished. Won't it look good?"

"Just two more loads of laundry. Then we'll be all set for the week. I'm sure glad to have clean clothes."

During the preschool years, it is not reasonable to expect a lot of quality work from our children. But they can help. When it's time to rake leaves, have fun. Let them rake, jump in the leaves, and spend time with Mom and Dad. Even if they mess up the yard more than they clean, help them learn to contribute.

As they reach kindergarten or first grade, children can be given some very simple jobs around the house like helping to clean their rooms, making their beds (not very neatly), picking up messes, helping prepare food, and setting the table.

By second or third grade, they are ready to do dishes, vacuum a room, take out trash, pick up sticks, wipe out the refrigerator, sweep the garage, or weed the garden. They are ready to be valuable contributors to the family.

Paying kids to do their chores robs them of the opportunity to feel like an important, contributing member of the family.

Some Love and Logic parents post a list of chores and let the kids decide which chores they would most like to do.

Some families take the time to develop a huge list of all the jobs necessary to keep the household going. It takes days to think of them all. Feed the dog. Earn the money. Wash dishes. Clean toilets. Go shopping. Paint beautiful pictures that can be displayed in the house.

After the list is complete, the family sits down to divide the work. Mom and Dad take a lot of jobs, and before long any kid worth his salt recognizes that fairness requires that the children also contribute. Everyone claims some chores, to be performed without reminders.

Some families post a special weekend list of chores as special projects come up. Once again, kids can negotiate or choose which chores are theirs, to be done by the end of the weekend.

**Give a child a job he can handle, then
hope and pray that he blows it.**

Some kids learn more easily than others. When Wendy forgot that Wednesday was her night for dishes, Mom just left them on the kitchen counter. Later Wendy noticed them.

"Oh, Mom. I'm sorry. I forgot. Should I do them now?"

"Yes, indeed."

Bert promised to take the trash to the curb on Wednesday night, but when bedtime came, he still didn't remember. His dad let him go to bed.

"Should I do it for him?" wondered Bert's dad. "I could make him do one of my chores tomorrow."

Then he noticed the snow beginning to fall. It was white and silent in the light of the front porch. It gave him peace as he decided.

Half an hour later he looked lovingly at his boy as he awakened him from a deep sleep.

"Dad. What is it? Is it time to get up?"

"Bert. Guess what?"

"What?"

"It's Wednesday night."

"Yeah?"

"What do you do on Wednesday night?"

Pausing, then realizing, "The trash."

"Good thinking."

"You mean now?"

"Yes, Bert. It's Wednesday night."

Watching Bert put on his boots and overcoat and trudge to the curb with the big trash barrel in the gently falling snow was a wondrous sight.

"Good night, Bert. Thanks. I love you."

**Even kids with challenging behaviors or attentional
challenges are capable of thinking ahead.**

"I'm not doing it. You can't make me do the dishes. I'm not a slave!" declared Marianne.

"That's so sad," said her mother. "Bad decision. I'm going to have to do something about that. Try not to worry about it. I'll get back to you."

Because she was just beginning to practice Love and Logic, Marianne's mother wasn't sure what to say, and she wasn't prepared to deal with her fourteen-year-old daughter at that moment. So she used the promise of an extended consequence.

She talked to her friends, and on Saturday she was ready. "I'm ready for our trip to the new mall," Mom announced.

"I'm ready," said ten-year-old Suzy.

"Me too," said Marianne.

Marianne's mother had been practicing for this moment. With genuine sadness she said, "Oh, Marianne. It's so sad. But don't worry, there will be other trips to the mall. Here's a list of chores you can do to make up for the energy I've put into doing your chores this week."

"You mean I can't come?"

"Not today. But look, here comes Mabel. She'll be here to make sure you get them done. Or maybe you could hire her to help. Good luck. Don't forget to discuss with Mabel how you're going to pay her."

It was a grand day of shopping and lunch. Suzy and her mom even decided to take in an afternoon movie.

Marianne's mom practiced avoiding lectures and threats on the way home. A new respect between mother and daughter was born that day.

Chores for the family teach respect for the family.

"Do you think you could clean up your mess in the garage before your next meal?" asked Nathan's mom.

"Sure, no problem," he blithely promised.

Now let's check. Are we hoping Nathan will have a sudden burst of responsibility and remember his promise? Or are we hoping he'll blow it off and have a significant learning experience?

The dinner table was only set for three, and Nathan's usual chair was removed when he came in for supper.

"What gives?" he asked.

"Oh Nathan. I guess you forgot that you were going to clean up the garage before your next meal."

"That's not fair. I forgot."

"I know," said his mom.

"This really stinks. This whole family stinks."

"Sorry you feel that way," said his mom. She didn't get pulled into an argument or lecture.

"It'll take me an hour to clean up that mess," pouted Nathan.

"I know," his mom agreed with sadness.

The ability to persevere, to give extra effort to important tasks, to anticipate how your choices will affect you, to feel valuable to your family—these are the gifts that come with doing regular chores for the family.

Rules for Chores

1. Avoid demanding, "Do It now!"
2. Provide a reasonable deadline, i.e., by the end of the day, before your next meal, by Friday night.
3. Plan your response if the chore is not done. Will you wake him up? Will he hire someone to do it for him? Will he hire someone to supervise his doing the job? If so, how will he pay?
4. Avoid reminders.

One wonderful mother worked with foster children. Sometimes they came to her in pretty rough shape. Once they were in her house, she gave them chores, and they began to feel valued.

Sometimes if her foster child was acting obstinate, she would sigh sweetly and remark, "Uh-oh. I feel an energy drain coming on."

Do your kids ever drain your energy by fighting, being rude, or disobeying?

A particularly tough boy explained why he had stopped disobeying.

"It's just not worth it. My mom says, 'Uh-oh. Energy drain,' and then I spend hours doing chores to make up for the energy I've drained from the family. It's just not worth it."

Only Good Minutes Are Spent in the Classroom

By the time you have established recovery time, control over food choices, and chores within the home, your child has begun to do work in school. He recognizes adults as caring authority figures in his life. He has begun to have many "good" minutes at school. These include minutes during which your child is not interfering with the learning of others. Listening and contributing to the class may also be happening.

As yet he may not be doing all his homework. Don't worry. We'll get to that. Now it's time to make sure that he's acting appropriately in school all day, not interfering with the work of others. After this is locked in, we will focus on his achievement and completion of school assignments.

"Mom, it's not my fault. That Mr. Stevenson just hates me," said David.

"It's sad you acted up today and can't stay at school."

"It's not my fault."

"Some kids think that way," said David's mom.

"What am I going to have to do?" asked David.

"I don't know yet. When we get home we'll look at the list of chores and figure it out."

"Do I have to pay you back for your driving time?"

"Yes."

"And your gas money?"

"Yes."

"And the use of your car?"

"Yes, David. But today I was going out to see a client, so you'll also get to pay Mabel for a couple of hours."

"I'm all out of money," he said sadly.

"You're not out of money until you have nothing left to take to the pawn shop."

(Later…)

"Mom, we've sure gotten a lot of chores done this month," said David.

"Yep, ever since we decided you are capable of handling a full school day. I don't think the house and yard have ever looked better."

"Mom, what are you going to do when I quit acting up at school? Who's going to do extra chores then?"

When your child is capable of spending a good day at school, it's appropriate for there to be a logical consequence if he makes a poor choice. But it's not enough. Even if you avoid using consequences with ranting, raving, and anger, consequences alone are never enough. *Logic* without *love* isn't enough to help your child become the wonderful human he's capable of being. It is also important at this stage of the Home Program to be sure you spend time and energy noticing the good things about your child. By working through the steps of the Home Program, your home has hopefully become a calmer, happier place. You have fun at meals. You are not afraid to take your brood out in public. You are treating yourself and your children with respect.

Positive Noticing is an application of attribution theory that many parents find effective:

"David, I've noticed that your writing is easier to read. I can read it so easily. What have you done to make that happen?"

"I don't know. I guess I'm not hurrying so much."

"What caused you to stop hurrying?"

"I don't know," said David thoughtfully.

"Well, it's very readable."

Helping our children notice the things they do well can be done in many ways.

"I noticed you were helping your sister with her reading. She certainly likes it when you help her."

Positive Noticing avoids effusive praise. The parent notices specific good behaviors and helps the child reflect on how that happened. It avoids generalized praise that may not be seen as truthful or accurate.

"You're just so wonderful with your sister," may not be seen as accurate or desirable by a ten-year-old boy. It is better to say, "I noticed you were helping your sister without yelling."

"Your writing is great," may not be seen as accurate and really doesn't help a child see any specific reason why the writing is good.

The process of helping your child feel capable of doing good school-work can be enhanced by noticing the schoolwork he does well. Try taking ten minutes twice a week to talk about school. Don't talk about the bad behavior reports. Don't focus on the mistakes that gave him a 63 percent on the math quiz. Instead, find and notice the work he's done well.

"David, can you show me an assignment you enjoyed? What was interesting about the assignment? What makes you like science? How long did it take you to finish? What do you think makes this such a great report?"

For these ten minutes ask questions and notice specific positive aspects of your child's work. Try not to digress into, "You're so wonderful." Keep it specific, and let your child decide that he's pretty darned good at schoolwork when he wants to be.

> **The things we give energy and attention
> to in our lives will grow. Ouch! That applies to
> the negative things as well.**

Homework

"You're doing pretty well at school these days."

"Yep."

"You're getting most of your assignments done, aren't you."

"Yep."

"Are you enjoying school?"

"Mostly."

"Bringing home your homework?"

"Mostly."

"You've made a lot of progress. I'm proud of you. And to help you get to be even more successful, I'm willing to give you half an hour of help every day (or any day you ask, if appropriate) for free."

"For free?" David asks suspiciously.

"Absolutely free," says David's dad.

"From now on, we'll expect you to get all your homework done and get decent grades. Every day I'll give you a half an hour of help getting organized and started, and then you can complete your study time on your own."

"What if I need more help?" asks David. "What if I need more than thirty minutes?"

"Great question. We've been working pretty hard on the Home Program, and half an hour will probably be enough help most days. But if you need more time than that, I'll be glad to take some of my resting time or family time and help you more."

"You're going to charge me aren't you?"

"You're learning. Anything over half an hour you can make up to me..."

David interrupted, "In chores. I know." He laughed. "What if I screw up and get lousy grades?"

"You're smart, David. And if you want you can earn good grades. I figure it's your choice if you want a C or a B or an A average. It's up to you. As long as you're passing all your classes, it's your choice. But if you decide to fail classes, then I'll be here to work with you. If needed, I'll supervise your entire daily study period."

"Oh, great," responded David. "And thirty minutes is free."

"Exactly," said his dad.

"So anything more than thirty minutes..."

"You've got it," exclaimed his dad.

"...I get to make up to you in chores."

The Home Program helps parents organize their efforts and deal with one behavior at a time. It helps parents establish themselves as firm, loving, authority figures. It helps a child begin to ask the question: How's my next decision going to affect me?

The Home Program

1. Neutralize arguments
2. Learn to use enforceable statements
3. Never break a sweat
4. Establish a routine for the first hour of the morning
5. Establish a working relationship with your child's teacher(s)
6. Develop a recovery time routine
7. Food issues
8. Chores
9. Only good minutes are spent in the classroom
10. Homework

Jim Fay and Bob Sornson

chapter eleven

The School Program

When Mr. and Mrs. Lorenz came in for their appointment, they were nervous. Schools make a lot of people nervous. After a moment of waiting they were ushered into the principal's conference room. It was filled with file cabinets and in the corner was an old 286 computer.

Mr. Cornfield and Ms. Samuelson, the principal and third grade teacher, were waiting for them. They were a little nervous, too. New parents to the school didn't often ask for appointments with both teacher and principal. And when they occasionally did, it was usually with a list of demands.

There was coffee in a pot on the table, and Mrs. Lorenz had baked some sweet rolls for the meeting. Perhaps, they all wondered, there is cooperation in the air.

Mrs. Lorenz began. "We wanted to tell you about Michael and about our family and the program we're using at home."

She explained about the Love and Logic book they'd been studying and the Home Program they were using. Mr. Lorenz told about Michael and about all the evaluations and heartache they'd been through. But now there was some hope. Michael's behavior was much improved, but not yet perfect. He was going to recovery time without coercion, and the food issues were almost eliminated at home.

"Do you think you could work with us?" asked Mr. Lorenz.

"We don't ever want him to interfere with the learning of the class," offered Mrs. Lorenz. "But we're finally making progress and we believe in Michael. If the school could help us along during the next few months, we're pretty sure he can be a good student."

And so it began. Most teachers and school administrators dream of helping kids and working with parents like the Lorenzes. The principal knew about Love and Logic, but not about the Home Program. Michael's teacher was eager to learn more, since it wasn't just Michael who would bring challenges to her classroom this year. Mr. and Mrs. Lorenz left a copy of this book for school staff to read as they embarked on the School Program.

Expect Students to Be in Class without Bothering Others

One great teacher in Montana has a red and white beach umbrella in the back of her room. It's in a little corner, a quiet place. There is a chair behind the umbrella. Kids who sit there can hear what's happening, but can't see or be seen. Occasionally, she'll walk near a child who's having a bad day and whisper so no one else can hear, "Do you need a little quiet time at the beach, or can you manage to stay with us and work?"

She has offered a respectful choice to a child who's struggling to hold things together. Who knows why he's struggling. Kids come to school with all kinds of worries and experiences. How can we expect them all to be ready for our instruction at any given moment? The "beach" is an alternative setting, not for punishment, but to allow a student a few moments to collect his thoughts or settle his emotions.

It doesn't require a beach umbrella. A quiet chair behind a screen, a cheery corner filled with posters from the Impressionists, or a fish tank and pictures of the Great Barrier Reef will do.

Some teachers make a deal with their teacher-friend down the hall. If you'll keep a chair in your room for a child who needs to be out of the class for a while, I'll do the same for you. Of course my student cannot be allowed to disrupt your class—just sit and collect her thoughts.

Many schools have a chair somewhere by the principal's office where kids can sit, but unfortunately it's usually associated with waiting for punishment. The recovery chair plan avoids the concept of punishment. It says to the student, "Feel free to be in school as long as you don't disturb the learning of others. If you are too upset (anxious, hyperactive, etc.) to learn at this moment, you can sit in the recovery chair until you are ready to learn."

Some schools even have a recovery room, where a trained staff member supervises thinking time until kids are ready to return to class. The recovery room is a place reserved for thinking, not doing assignments and not listening to adult lectures.

For some children on some days, school is not a place where they can be without making it hard for others to learn. On those days, it's appropriate to say, "We love you too much to let you have bad minutes in school. We hope to see you tomorrow."

In a few schools, there are times when older students may be given a choice. "The good folks at the nursing home (or church, township, cemetery, etc.) have offered to let students who are having a bad day come over and work for the rest of the day instead of going home. Do you think that might work for you?"

Love and Logic schools have strict standards, but also remember to offer consequences with empathy rather than anger.

Develop Relationships with Parents and Students

Can you think of the teachers you admire most and who helped you learn the most? It is likely that these revered teachers treated students with respect, had high expectations, and helped you see something special about yourself.

Children with challenging behaviors or attentional challenges will respond to teachers who use thinking words rather than fighting words, communicate high expectations, and notice specific positive behaviors.

For many challenging students there is one special adult that comes along and changes their lives. Somehow this adult sees that unique and wondrous quality within them. Students will work harder for an adult they love. Think about it. Would you rather study with an instructor who possesses technical knowledge of her subject, or one that makes you feel uniquely gifted as a human being? The great teacher can actually do both.

> **When a student loves and respects a teacher,**
> **that student will give enormous effort to stay in class**
> **and continue to enjoy that respect.**

Relationships with parents are also important. If a child knows that the adults in his life are in regular communication, respect one another, and support each other's efforts, better learning occurs.

Develop a Foolproof Reporting System

Once the first eight steps of the Home Program are in place, the student is ready to be responsible for completion of work at school and homework. For the parents to be able to complete steps 9 and 10, a foolproof reporting system is needed.

These parents have worked hard and need our support to complete the job. For many students, the use of an assignment book provides a good communication tool. Some students can fill it out on their own. Others need a peer-coach to check it each day. Still others need an adult to check the book before leaving school for home.

> **For many kids, a foolproof reporting system includes**
> **an understanding that if the child brings home no report from the**
> **teacher, then additional study time is needed.**

Over time, we hope to withdraw adult support from the homework process, but this decision is a collaborative one involving both teacher and parent.

Occasionally, a student needs a behavior log or points chart. If the student's parents are working through the Home Program, please give them all the support and information they need to follow through at home. The use of behavior logs or point charts should be temporary.

A regular phone call, conferences when needed, even an email of encouragement is worthwhile when helping a parent who is learning to help a challenging child accept responsibility.

Find Good Reasons to Let Kids Move

Some children need to move during the school day. Sitting quietly, holding their muscles still, not stimulating their kinesthetic and vestibular systems for hours at a time is torture. When you notice those children, find positive ways to let them move.

"Fred, would you please go pet the bunny. He looks a little bit lonely."

"Margaret, please take this heavy stack of books to Mrs. Gallagher's office. Tell her they're from me."

"Jack, run down and find the custodian and tell him I'll be needing my room cleaned again tonight."

"Sally, would you try sitting on this wiggler seat today and tell me if it's worth purchasing?"

"Rachel, would you like to practice reading today while standing on my new balance board?"

"Marty, it's time to walk around the school again and see if any geese are on the playground. Remember to fill in the chart when you return."

Apply Attribution Theory

Those things we notice and give energy to will grow, so help students notice their specific positive behaviors or characteristics.

"You were really concentrating on that science project today. Can you tell me about that?"

"Thanks for helping Rachel on the playground. You often seem to notice kids in need. Why is that?"

"You use descriptive words in your writing. How did you learn that?"

"Wow. 90 percent on math again. You've certainly improved your math skills. Do you have any secrets for your improvement?"

"You've been controlling your talking for an hour. What did you do to make that happen?"

By noticing specific good behaviors and asking the child to help you understand, the child notices, thinks, and begins to look at himself from a new perspective.

Remember that noticing positive behaviors is not enough. Encourage the child to identify and express the reasons for his/her success.

Frequent use of this technique causes the child to develop a stronger focus of self-control and a more positive self-concept. It helps students perceive that they can cause positive outcomes by their own choices or efforts.

Use Positive Peer Pressure/The Egg Timer

Some teachers with one or more challenging students have found success using variable schedules of reinforcement. One teacher puts a penny in a jar at varied intervals if the class is on task. When there are enough pennies, the class enjoys a pizza party. Another uses jelly beans in a different manner. He takes one jelly bean and enjoys eating it when the class is doing great work. "It's a jelly bean moment," he announces. When the jar is empty, the class gets a reward.

Some teachers like to use an egg timer. It's quiet, except when it rings. They set it to go off at different intervals. If everyone is behaving, one tally mark is awarded to the class. Each tally mark is worth one minute of reward. Older kids often choose visiting time. Younger students usually like playground time.

Marks are never taken away for bad behavior. "That's so sad. Don't worry, I'll reset the timer."

Teachers who use this method recommend never giving more or less reward time than earned. Some teachers report that once they have established the process, they allow a student with attentional challenges to set the timer.

We get control by sharing control.

Give Positive Parent Feedback

The teachers who make ten positive phone calls for every one negative call they must make are my heroes. They know that to have a good relationship wherein parents can occasionally listen to bad news, they must have at least ten positive interactions for each time the news is crummy. Even the most dedicated parent and friend of the school gets tired of hearing bad news.

Mrs. Doheny makes two positive calls per day. She's never phony. She shares a little story about your child and there are no "buts." By sharing a positive story or observation she builds a belief that she notices the good in your child, which every parent longs to know. If she ever needs to call about a problem, a relationship has already been established.

Mr. Anderson likes to catch kids doing good and sends an "I caught you" note home whenever possible. Mrs. Gullen likes random acts of kindness. She builds a tree in her room made of leaves. Each leaf tells about a random act of kindness she observed in her room. She sends a copy of each leaf home.

Celebrate the successes of your students at school, and share those successes with their parents.

Imagine It Working

Sometimes it's hard to imagine. There are so many more kids today who seem to have difficulty sustaining attention. There are so many kids with challenging behaviors.

By reading this book, perhaps you have begun to imagine parents and teachers working together, holding kids accountable in a loving way, avoiding fighting words and building relationships, using choices and enforceable statements, helping kids learn to solve problems in a way that does not make a problem for others.

As teachers, you have dedicated your lives to working with children and their families. Your greatest reward is helping kids grow into positive human beings. By sharing the ideas in this book, you can help educators and parents develop a common plan and the skills needed to help children become truly successful. Imagine it working.

The School Program

1. Expect students to be in class without bothering others
2. Develop relationships with parents and students
3. Develop a foolproof reporting system
4. Find good reasons to let kids move
5. Apply Attribution Theory
6. Use positive peer pressure
7. Give positive parent feedback
8. Imagine it working

chapter twelve

How to Communicate Effectively with Your School

Some parents are so scared to death when they enter a school to discuss their child's progress. Old memories of authority figures from times past and sometimes fears or failures accompany them through the door. They may appear to be quiet, or at times, they may become abrasive.

Some parents are so busy that a school request for a meeting is very inconvenient. They just know that the teacher or principal is going to ask them to fit one more job into an already overwhelming life. There's work, cooking, cleaning, soccer, piano, scouts, basketball, and Tae Kwon Do. They're exhausted, and their lives are not going the way they dreamed, and their kids are slightly out of control. *And you want what?*

Most parents would do anything in the world to help their children become happy, healthy, ethical human beings. But, sometimes we are confused. It's not always clear how to handle family and child-rearing issues. There are no networks of support for many parents. Our families are spread across the country. No more uncles, aunts, and grandparents ready to straighten you out when you screw up. Many people aren't involved in church communities. Neighbors are afraid to discipline your kids, and people move so often. Many parents feel isolated and unsure of the quality of their parenting.

And some parents are angry when they come to school. Countless educators have told me stories about angry parents. These teachers feel hurt and distressed. They want to be helping people. They're not trained to deal with anger.

When you get that call from the school, it's usually about a problem. Don't ask me why. In the next chapter, we'll discuss ways for the school to improve relationships and establish working partnerships with parents. My advice to you is this: *Don't wait for the call.*

There are so many reasons for parents to reach out and establish a good relationship with their child's teacher and school. Research by James Comer and others shows that parent involvement in the school is related to student success. We're talking PTAs, parent conferences, family fun nights, and parent education programs. And Dads, the research specifically states that your involvement is important. This is not a task to be delegated.

High expectations are also related to student success, and that certainly means you want to communicate what's special about your child to her teacher. But it's more than that. High expectations of teacher performance by the student and her parents is also related to success. The expectation of success is a complex relationship involving teachers, parents, principals, and children. It assumes an atmosphere of respect and trust. Snide, angry, or distrustful remarks undermine that respect and trust.

Many children leave for school each morning thinking, "How can I be expected to learn when I have such a bad teacher?" Guess where they get this notion? It's from hearing their parents complain about school.

Many kids carry the same contempt for schools that their parents express. The fortunate kids are ones who hear appreciation for and belief in teachers.

It is unwise to discuss even the most legitimate concerns about our schools in front of the kids.

When children know that the adults respect each other and are working together, there is far less opportunity to play one side against another.

When Billy reports, "Guess what? This year the school has moved to a new grading process. Less paperwork. No more of those ten-week reports." As parents you can respond, "Nice try, Billy boy. But we're not buying it."

Don't wait for problems to develop. Establish relationships of trust and communication. One brilliant set of parents was moving to our district. The mother called me up, then followed her call by this (slightly altered) letter to her daughter's new teachers.

Dear Teachers:

Please let us introduce ourselves. We have recently moved into your district, and our daughter Sally will be a student in your class. Sally has been diagnosed as having attention deficit disorder without hyperactivity. We would like to share some information with you, which we hope will help Sally be successful in your class. Along with this letter, we include a report from Dr. Mel Levine, which contains a few practical suggestions that significantly help Sally to achieve more in school.

Our primary goals for Sally this school year include:

• Helping her to understand how she learns best.
• Developing organizational skills and habits that will serve her as a lifelong learner.
• Maintaining the love of learning that she generally displays.

Our biggest concern is that Sally might feel overwhelmed in a new school environment and that she might fall into a pattern of disorganization, causing a lack of success in school without our awareness.

Because Sally has to work much harder than most students to stay organized, we want to be aware of any difficulties she is having in school so we may help her maintain a positive attitude.

Sally has many resources away from school. First among these is her family. Both of us are willing to take time in the evening to help Sally with assignments, and her older brother has frequently taken time to proofread papers or essays. Each Saturday Sally sees a tutor. This will continue at least through the end of this school year. Her tutor works with Sally to help her get organized and to break down difficult tasks into manageable chunks. Additionally, Sally takes medication twice a day for her attention deficit. This medication helps her stay at a higher level of attention during the work hours of her day. It is not clear to us at this time if she will need to continue to be medicated as an adult.

We have several requests for adaptations within the class that we know can help Sally be successful. These include:

1. Please have her sit near the front of the classroom, or if that is impossible, seat her next to a strong, positive role model who can demonstrate good organization skills and good attention in class.

2. You're probably already doing this, but for Sally it is especially important that any assignments be written down, either on the blackboard or on paper. Sometimes, just hearing an assignment is not enough for Sally.

3. Sally is very responsible, but please let us know if she falls more than two assignments behind in your class, or fails two tests in a row. We do not want to take the responsibility for her test preparations or assignment completion from her, and if she fails on a particular assignment, please deal with her directly. However, we do have a concern that any pattern of failures might require intervention on our part, so please keep us informed.

4. It would be very helpful if any long-term assignments like research projects or major projects of any kind be broken down for Sally into specific, concrete steps. A timeline for completion would be particularly helpful.

5. Sally needs at least one adult at school whom she feels she can talk to openly—a mentor who can help her set appropriate goals in school and give feedback on her progress and interaction at school. This person can be a counselor or a teacher. Please consider this request and let us know your ideas.

6. If ever there is a prescribed change in Sally's level of medication, we will notify you. If that should occur, we will ask you to watch for and report any changes in mental alertness.

7. Please encourage Sally to ask for help in the class. Sometimes she is shy about this.

8. Sally needs extra time for written tests. She organizes information more slowly, and she writes very slowly. You will not be able to ascertain how much Sally really knows in a time-limited testing situation.

9. Do you ever allow alternative forms of assessment for students? Sally is very creative, and if there is an opportunity for her to do a photo journal, an oil painting, a three-dimensional model, or some other demonstration of understanding rather than a written assignment, she will be able to show you some of her other skills while clearly indicating her understanding of the subject matter.

In summary, Sally is a wonderful daughter who works with consistency and persistence. She is good with people and good with her hands. Sally learns well through movement and through direct experience. Her attention and organizational needs will probably be with her for her whole life. To deal with these she needs to learn "how to learn," "how to organize," and "how to set goals." We hope that with your help she will maintain the love of learning and the confidence in herself that she has today.

If you need to contact either of us, you can reach us at work or at home. My work number is (810) 123-0000, between 8:00 A.M. and 4:30 P.M. Paul's schedule includes trips out of town, but his work number is (810) 123-0001. We can almost always be reached at home after 6:00 P.M. at (810) 123-1111. Thank you for your consideration. We look forward to meeting with you in the near future.

Sincerely,

Anne and Paul Smith

Some parents develop relationships with school staff by spending time in their child's elementary class as a helper and noticing the good things that are occurring. Some parents volunteer to help at lunchtime, even in middle schools or high schools. Some parents send notes when they have seen an especially creative or well designed assignment.

Some parents seem to naturally understand the 10-to-1 rule. It took me a long while to figure it out. When I was a special education teacher at Petoskey High School, I noticed that a few students were not making progress like the others. It bothered me, and I began to observe more carefully.

One kid in particular was annoying to me. He was a sneaky little weasel, with a terrible complexion, body odor, and a whiny voice. I had fewer positive interactions with this fellow than most of the others. I had to bark at him or give negative feedback a little more. I made a chart.

I noticed that when I charted three positive interactions for every negative interaction, he was still pretty churlish. When I increased to seven positive interactions for each negative (this took great effort), he was still annoying and not very motivated. I persisted. At ten positive interactions for every negative interaction something profound began to occur. He was listening more. His whining stopped. It became easier to notice good behaviors.

My positive interactions with him were not that profound. A touch on the shoulder, a genuine smile, noticing new shoes, noticing an interesting use of language on a writing assignment. False or insincere compliments were not counted on the positive side.

When I slipped a little and sank below the 10-to-1 ratio, his churlish demeanor returned. The same held true in my relationships with other students. What a discovery, I congratulated myself. Pure genius, I concluded. But as I shared my discovery with others, the sad truth began to emerge. Lots of others already knew about the 10-to-1 rule. Coaches have known about it for years. Athletic training is improved when athletes spend time in an appropriate training range, with just the right balance of challenge and expectation of success. When a task becomes too difficult to predict success, motivation decreases, enjoyment decreases, and learning decreases.

Great teachers have always known about the 10-to-1 rule. Ed Gickling did research with first graders learning to read. When they knew 93–97 percent of the words and concepts being used in their lesson, their time on task, motivation, and learning were optimal. Over 97 percent was too easy, and they were a little bored. Under 90 percent was too frustrating to sustain effort. Great instruction is like riding the edge of a wave, with just the right balance of challenge and stability. At a ski resort, skiers seek the hills that offer just the right balance of challenge and security. In their play activities, children select games that challenge them just enough to make it exciting.

The 10-to-1 rule also applies to parent-teacher relationships, and probably to relationships in general. Who are we willing to really listen to, even if their observations might be negative? Most people reject criticism from people they don't trust. Only when we have a relationship that has grown through positive interactions will we be open to really listening to difficult information. Who are the people in your life you would invite to tell you what you're doing wrong?

And yet so often parents and educators forget the importance of building relationships before we offer to point out what the other person is doing wrong.

·······♥·······

chapter thirteen

What Schools Can Do to Help

One scenario goes like this. Johnny is having a difficult time staying focused and behaving appropriately in first grade. His parents are not sure what to do. The negative reports they are getting from school add to their distress. After a few months, they conclude the teacher hates their son. Their own parenting skills are being questioned. They feel defensive, and they've begun to bicker at home. Dad feels Mom is too lenient. Mom thinks Dad is unreasonably harsh at times.

By fourth grade, the home-school relationship is suffering. Johnny is doing terribly in school, and home life is not much better. By fifth grade the parents have found an advocate that helps them blame the school for all of Johnny's troubles. He should be in special education, or have a 504 plan. Somehow the parents have come to believe that having Johnny officially acknowledged as being handicapped would require the system to treat him better and quit blaming the parents for his behavior. After many threats and angry meetings, Johnny is certified. A written contract says Johnny can do less work and turn it in late. Someone else will take notes for him and write down any daily assignments. At last, the schools have acknowledged that Johnny is handicapped. Johnny, too, has gotten the message. In eighth grade, he beats up another student, who is injured badly enough to go to the hospital. Surely

Johnny's impulsivity is to blame. The advocate argues he should not be disciplined. What is Johnny learning now?

· · · · ·

In another scenario, the school decided to work proactively with students who have attentional challenges and challenging behaviors and their parents. They began to work out a plan.

Recognizing the importance of **building relationships** between school and parents to enhance the school success of students, the teachers and principals began to emphasize relationships like never before. Teachers got more involved in PTA. Classroom teachers and the school principal sent home regular newsletters.The district provided training to help them write positive, succinct messages.

The teaching staff decided together to **improve parent-teacher conference opportunities.** They sent home a letter inviting parents to arrange a conference any time they saw a need. Within one week of a request, the teacher would arrange a mutually convenient time to meet. Warm beverages would be provided.

Teachers began searching for ways to build opportunities for **positive communication** so they could implement the 10-to-1 rule. Some wrote notes. Some made calls to report happy and wonderful observations.

At the teachers' request, the district hired a consultant to train them in the use of **listening skills.** They learned to ask questions rather than offer information at the beginning of a parent conference. What have you observed this school year? Does your child like to come to school? Do you have any concerns? What would you like to see your child accomplish this year?

After receiving input from the parents, they learned to check for understanding. "Let's see if I've got it … Is that correct?" Only after soliciting input, listening to parents, and checking for understanding did they offer advice or information.

They found this a very effective way to move parents from the emotional state to the thinking state. Parents became better listeners as teachers became better listeners.

"Would you like to hear some of my observations?" the teacher might ask. If the parents still needed to discuss their concerns, the teachers learned to be patient and wait until the parents were ready. Then once again, the teacher might ask, "Would you like to hear some of my observations?" This is in contrast to the oft-used statement, *"Let me tell you what that kid of yours did this week!"*

To further **build relationships between school and the whole family,** time and effort were devoted to developing family fun nights, math nights, science fun for the family, Dad Days, Grandparent Days, Moms and Music Days. Staff looked forward to participating in these events to develop a loving relationship between real people at home and school.

After great debate, the school board decided its mission needed to be adjusted. No longer could the education of students between kindergarten and twelfth grade be its only focus. To be truly successful with students, the school board needed to incorporate a greater emphasis on family needs into its mission.

Many student success issues were family issues. Developing terrific parenting skills at home, knowing how to prepare your child during the preschool years, knowing how to support early reading and math training at home, learning ways to structure homework and practice learning time, learning about the relationship between motor-skill development and school success for young children, learning how to prevent substance abuse, learning how music training affects early learning, and learning how home schedules and structure especially affect children with attentional problems are all directly related to success at school. The school board decided it could no longer act in isolation from parents and families. If parents are our partners, let's give them every opportunity to develop the skills they need to enhance the lives of their beautiful children. Providing quality **parent learning** opportunities became an important part of the district's purpose.

After careful analysis, the teaching staff and principals decided that every educational improvement they could

**make to help students with attentional needs was an
improvement that would benefit all students.**

They began to learn **Love and Logic techniques** to provide firm limits
while developing **positive relationships with students.** Of course, they
also noticed that these techniques helped create an atmosphere of respect
in the school and helped students become better problem solvers.

Teachers began practicing the use of **Attribution Theory** by noticing
and mentioning one or two personal or positive things about each
student each day. This was tough at first. Gradually, they became better
at avoiding general comments like "Nice job" or "Good effort" and
began to be more specific. "I noticed you were really listening during
story time today." "I noticed you got eight out of ten right. How did
you do that?" "You kept running for seven full minutes during gym
today. That's two more minutes than last week." Of course this kind of
noticing by teachers helped them implement **the 10-to-1 rule,** which
further improved their **relationships with students.**

As the teachers studied how to improve movement opportunities for
students with attention problems, they reviewed the research on regular
cardiovascular activity and found that it enhanced learning and
reduced behavioral problems for all students. They debated whether
to increase physical education time or to incorporate cardiovascular
activity into the classroom schedule.

They also discovered in the research and by observation that some
children with learning difficulties have **motor skill development** delays.
Of course, so did some children with attention problems, some of
whom were also struggling in school. The P.E. and classroom teachers
worked together, and involved parents to help design plans to enhance
the development of these fundamental skills.

An interesting debate developed. The school was attempting to **offer
support services to any child who needed them,** as early as possible, to
avoid learning failure. In the old days, kids had to struggle for years and
get one and one-half or two standard deviations behind the achievement

scores of their peers before they were given support services. These teachers didn't want their students to experience years of failure before they could get help.

The teachers analyzed the problem. So did the administration. So did the school board. What they realized was that by providing **support services early** they could significantly improve early learning success and permanently cut down on expensive special education placements. In a few years, they'd be saving millions of dollars annually.

Not just children with motor-skill delays were being helped. Some of the children with attention problems had **visual processing** difficulties. They strained their eyes when reading or doing table work. They lost their place when reading. Some saw double. They began to get help.

Some children had **auditory processing** or language development delays. The speech teachers and classroom teachers worked together to serve them. In many of the primary grade classrooms, sound-field amplification devices were used to help with auditory attention, discrimination, and language development.

By developing relationships with their students, using class meetings, and teaching conflict-resolution skills, the teachers had developed classrooms in which every student felt **care.** By helping every student find success, diversifying instruction within the class so every child could do something challenging yet possible (the 10-to-1 rule), the students felt **competent.** By using Love and Logic techniques like the controlled use of choices and the five-step problem-solving process, students felt **control** over their own destiny. These three "C"s, **Care, Competence,** and **Control,** are the building blocks of personal motivation.

Of course, the teachers began to review the application of recent research on brain function to instructional practice. They clearly noticed the **variance of attentional problems** noted by Dr. Mel Levine, Dr. Daniel Amen, and others. They consciously practiced **varying instructional technique** so that children with auditory, visual, or kinesthetic attentional preferences each had an opportunity to learn using their strength for a portion of each day. The multiple intelligence research by Howard Gardner was used to further understand learning preferences, and Anthony Gregorc's work was studied to better understand reasoning and organizational styles.

The teachers concluded that there is such incredible variance in thinking and learning styles that every area of learning demanded varied approaches to instruction. They even decided that great learning was more important than great teaching. Part of the research on great learning said that **relating new learning to what we already know,** and **understanding that something is worth learning** are both needed for long-term retention. Then they discussed mastery. Good instruction usually begins when students know 80 to 90 percent of the words and concepts being used. Could they use 80 percent on a written test to determine mastery and then expect that kids would retain and use that information? I guess not.

Teachers started spending more time **preteaching,** drawing relationships between new information and what children already knew. Then they taught to real mastery. They **retaught using different instructional methods** to anyone who wasn't getting it. Then did they move on to another lesson?

No. Then it was time to **practice using new ideas** and information in interdisciplinary activities, demonstrations, and projects. Music, drama, and other forms of artistic expression were integrated into lessons and projects. Only after mastery and extended use could teachers assume all the students would remember.

Since they were spending more time creating opportunities for deep and extended learning, teachers had to evaluate the amount of stuff their curriculum or textbook was trying to cover. They learned that the 1997 Third International Math and Science Study (TIMSS) clearly recommended **covering less "stuff," but teaching and learning what they did cover better.**

Teachers looked at their old tendency to teach like gangbusters for fifty minutes, then stop, switch subjects, and teach like mad in another direction for the next fifty minutes. Since they were quickly moving toward **interdisciplinary** and **thematic instruction** already, it wasn't too hard when they moved to **longer blocks of instruction** with structured **breaks for movement and relaxation.** The emotional conditions for great learning were beginning to occur. **Joy** was usually present in the classroom.

When teachers get moving on a path of great learning, it's hard to stop them. They looked at the nutritional needs of students with attention problems and then looked at the fast food school lunch program. At the elementary schools they requested a more nutritious, if slightly more expensive, menu. They offered parent education and tried to modify their old snack and reinforcement systems. At the middle and high schools, they tried to find a balance between more nutritious foods and student choice.

Somebody read one of Dr. Doris Rapp's books and began to wonder if the school environment wasn't affecting some children poorly. Along with maintenance staff, teachers evaluated the need for purified water, safer cleaning products, full spectrum lighting, and air cleaning systems.

Still there were some children that needed more time to complete assignments, or strategic seating near the front of the class or next to a student who modeled good organization skills. These **adaptations** were **freely given** to any student who needed them. The adaptations that helped were written down on an **Adaptation Plan** (Appendix 1) so that future teachers could know what helped.

And that got some of them thinking. Why just pass this information along to next year's teacher? All year long I've been learning how this group of children learns best and creating wonderful relationships. Perhaps I should move along to the next grade with them so that everyone doesn't have to start from scratch in August. And so some teachers began "looping," following their students from one grade to the following grade.

Some teachers created a special place within their classrooms. They called this place "The Beach" or "Australia" or "Bora Bora." Students who were having a rough day were sometimes asked, "Do you need to spend a little time in **Bora Bora** today to get yourself calm and relaxed?" It was not a place of punishment.

Teachers at all levels began including **social skill development** into their units. Some of the kids with attention problems really needed these skills. So did others.

In the later elementary grades and throughout middle school, teachers helped their students develop **organizational skills** and habits of learning. By the end of middle school, each student could explain how he/she learned best in different types of learning situations and what daily habits they were developing to help them be successful lifelong learners (see Appendix 2).

The school in this example has become a learning community, with staff sharing information, seeking new ideas, and modeling lifelong learning for their students. More and more the school is filled with joy. Love and Logic, positive relationships, attribution theory, the 10-to-1 rule, cardiovascular exercise, motor-skill training, support services available early, including visual and auditory process development, the 3 "C"s, varied instructional techniques, reteaching for all who need it, relating instruction to what we already know, helping kids understand why a subject is worth learning, practicing the use of new ideas, teaching less but teaching it better, lots of joy, nutrition, looping, safe schools, adaptations freely given, Bora Bora, social skills, organizational skills, and teachers modeling a love of learning have all become part of the culture of the school in this second scenario. Which scenario would you choose for your child with attention problems?

chapter fourteen

Never Let Your Child Be a Victim

Advantages and Disadvantages to Victimhood

There are many people who play victim in the United States. If it were not a common problem, we would not be talking about it here. To be honest, there are advantages to one's believing that he or she is a victim of circumstances. People may relate to victims by feeling sorry for them, and there is a good chance that victims can then manipulate the situations. Victims do this through playing on another's guilt or sense of obligation. Nobody likes to say "no" to a victim.

But the disadvantages of feeling victimized outweigh the advantages. Victimization as a lifestyle has been raised to an art form in the United States. If we slip on the ice, it is someone else's fault. If we spill coffee on ourselves, it is the fault of the restaurant that served the coffee too hot. Victims can hopefully use their situation as an excuse for nonachievement. And "playing victim" in America can certainly bring in big bucks.

But there are problems, too. Knowledge that one is "disadvantaged" does nothing at all to increase one's self-image or sense of accomplishment or encourage good changes in behavior.

We *never* want our children with A.D.H.D. or other labels to feel or think they are victims of circumstances. Why not?

- Victims are powerless.
- Victims always resent those with more power and may be consumed by jealousy and hate.
- Feelings of victimization always turn simple anger into rage. Rage is a combination of anger, helplessness, and hopelessness.
- People who feel victimized have no hope of bettering their own situation by their own actions.

Banishing Victimhood by Giving the "Can Do" Message

Even when children are victims of circumstances, it is best if parents give their children the "can-do message." I remember seeing this when I was making a home visit where a great foster mom was about to leave her house to take a physically handicapped child who also had A.D.H.D. for a doctor's appointment. We had been standing on the driveway talking, and her boy David, ten, had been wriggling around in the backseat. She was seated in the car talking through the open window to me, and as the time for leaving drew near, she attempted unsuccessfully to start her vehicle. I knew the appointment was important and I wondered what this mom would do. She certainly had to do something! But she solved it, to my utter amazement, by dropping the whole problem on her foster son: "David," she said, somewhat firmly, "the car won't start, now what are you going to do?" I could hardly believe it. It was her problem and she had just deftly dropped it on her "poor kid"! But this little boy stopped wriggling, opened the car door and rose *on his crutches* to say, "Well, I'd better call someone, maybe Mr. Edwards."

She smiled at me and said, "I'm working on raising his self-image, so I'm helping him make things happen for *both* of us!"

Parents unknowingly give their children a feeling of victimization whenever they imply that when bad things happen in their lives, there is someone else to blame for how they feel about the situation.

The truth is, life *is* unfair. For our special children, it may be particularly unfair. Sometimes children with attention problems set themselves apart by being impulsive and loud or obnoxious and negative. Sometimes slightly slow kids are called "stupid" or "dummy." When kids look different, they are called "ugly" and when they wear thick glasses, they are called "coke eyes." Children can't control how others treat them, but *with the help of Love and Logic techniques, parents can usually ensure that their children are not stuck in a victim life stance.*

Some parents of special children do not encourage their children to feel like victims:

Robin, eleven, had a somewhat disturbed (and disturbing) fifth grade teacher with fairly obvious personality problems. And her parents told her, "Boy are you lucky. Some people have to wait until they are adults to learn how to deal with a real wacky person. But lucky for you, you are learning how at eleven! And if you can learn to handle Mr. Smithson, you can learn to handle anybody!"

Robert knew he was different. His parents told him with quite some enthusiasm that he was a special random, nonlinear thinker. And that was something pretty "unique." When teachers felt exasperated with Rob, he would sometimes look at them solemnly and explain to them that he understood it was frustrating, but that he was a unique random, nonlinear thinker, and somehow as teacher's smiled, everything seemed to calm down.

When Larry was a child he had a severe motor output problem. In those days, when children did their schoolwork slow and messy they were considered "dumb." Fast and neat writers were considered smart. No one looked at learning styles and strengths when Larry went to school in the 1940s and 1950s. He was put into slower classes. And he complained to his mom that he was very bored in class. As well he might be, because the work that was expected was far beneath Larry's comprehension level. He understood things completely, he just didn't know how to "show" it.

Larry's mom always gave him special things to figure out for her while he was at school. And it was those things with which he occupied his mind during classes where he might otherwise have vegetated out. How many minutes left until the end of the year? How many holes in the drop ceiling of the entire school? This of course meant counting the holes in one ceiling panel, multiplying by the number of panels in the room, then by the number of classrooms in the school. Years later, he mused, "I think my mom could have gotten me out of several of those classes, but I'm certainly no worse for it, and I'm never bored in airports!"

So, *in handling tough times, it is not the victimizing incidents that parents must prevent. Those will happen no matter what. It is making sure that the children have the correct attitude when facing these events.* Wise parents give their children the strength to cope with problems. They don't try to remove the problem! It is the attitude that parents should be concerned about, not stopping the event!

In my years of practice, I've seen many kids who justified not doing well in school because they were "gifted and bored." And I always knew where that one came from—right from the parents.

After relating to the children for a bit, I would always ask if they ever thought psychiatrists got bored. They all said that they thought probably so. Then I would ask them if they thought I could be bored seeing them. And most of them thoughtfully allowed as to how that might easily be the case! But I always noted that I did a great job with them whether I was bored or not.

Children understand drawings and metaphors if explained by the adults. Most of Hans Christian Anderson's fairytales were designed for lonely "different" little kids who might feel like an ugly ducking in the chicken yard.

With a kid sitting on my lap, I like to use my favorite metaphor with the special children.

I understand that times are tough for you right now. It reminds me of how times always get tough for ingots of iron. The iron gets thrown into white hot flame, and times get tough for the iron, just as it is tough for you right now with the other kids making fun of you. That burns you, I know. And the ingots burn too. But an amazing thing happens to that old iron.

You see, iron is brittle and really not good for much. But when that iron is heated and gets really hot... if it doesn't break, it comes out steel. Strong as you can ever imagine. Some of the iron breaks, but most of it comes out steel. And it is so valuable and sharp that great swords and other stuff is made out of it that people want more than anything else.

And that's what may happen to you. You are in a tough, hot, difficult situation, but if you don't break, you could come out...

"Steel," says the kid.

Yes, and you will be sharper and understand things other's don't, and you will be super valuable to all the people around you. When the going gets tough, the tough get going. Do you think you are more likely to break or more likely to come out valuable steel?

Nine out of ten kids leave the office feeling "sharp like steel." And when the one-in-ten says he or she may break, I put that back on the child too, saying, that could be, but it would surprise me, because he or she looks like one of kids who could ultimately handle it.... And almost all of them ultimately do!

Banishing Victimhood by Concentrating on the Child's Strengths

Almost every child has an area of strength that adults can focus on and encourage. Remember that it is only in childhood that people are exhorted to remediate their deficits!

The ineffectiveness of the way many parents relate to their children can be seen if we imagine adults talking that way to each other around adult accomplishments:

Most husbands would not do well to say to their wives, "Dear, the house looks pretty good, I would say it is a 'C' job, which would be fine if that was the best you could do. But with a little more effort and a little more time, this place could look like an 'A' job!"

"George, I liked your financial report to the company, but it could have been better . . . and you have so much potential!"

Most wives would not do well to say to their husbands, "This car looks really clean. Now that I know you can do a job like this cleaning off the seats and floors, I'm going to expect it like this all the time."

In adulthood we usually do *not* look around, find things we don't do well or don't enjoy and then concentrate on improving them. Instead, as adults, we generally do things because we enjoy them or because we are good at them. Most adults pick out things they enjoy doing in the first place and *then* work to improve them! In childhood, we often ask children to improve in areas they don't enjoy. To be honest, I have run into some adults who are forever trying to remediate the things they do wrong, rather than concentrate on their strengths, but they have not been effective, fulfilled, happy campers!

However, most adults improve on subjects for the joy of it, whether it is fishing, writing, building, teaching, or attempting to try more than 500 different substances as filaments to burn in an incandescent lamp, as did Thomas Edison. William Russell loved painting and kept on getting better at it every year.

Far from remediating deficits, the average adult, like the wise parents of children with attentional challenges, find ways to *work around* the deficit and concentrate on the strengths.

Eddie seemed to be good at one thing. That was taking things apart! His mom went to secondhand stores and garage sales. Eddie had a never-ending supply of clocks and watches to take apart.

"Well, it saves the clock on the mantle, if nothing else," chuckled his mom.

Foster Cline had fairly severe perceptual motor problems as a child. He did poorly in school until his eighth grade teacher, placing a hand on his shoulder, told him, "You are no good on paper, but you have a good mouth," and invited him to take the eighth grade speech and drama class. What a difference concentrating on his strengths made! He often credited his junior high teacher, Jack D'Arcy, for helping him both feel good about school and start him on his path toward the skills he needed to become an internationally-known speaker. He is still looking for ways around his deficits and married a woman who is waiting for the price of Global Positioning Devices to come down so she can replace the compass he needs to find his way around the block!

In his small classroom with six other kids, Eric's teacher, Jane, allowed him to work on the floor. Sometimes under his desk! When a visitor showed some surprise at this, she laughed, "Hey, I just want the work done. He's just one of those kids who does it better halfway upside down."

Children with attention, learning or behavior problems do live, in some ways, a tougher life than many other children. They can learn to accept themselves the way they are, if *we, as parents, accept them for who they are.* When we don't look at children as victims, but as special creatures of God with unique gifts, we focus on the child's strengths. When we give the kids a "can do" attitude, they grow into adulthood feeling good about themselves and the contributions they will make.

chapter fifteen

Jimmy

She watched them intently as they raced around the playground. Jimmy's blue jacket was open, and it flapped as he ran. Two of the other boys ran after him, yelling, with angry looks. Mrs. Peterson sighed, then started walking out to meet them.

Jimmy was fast. All the kids knew it, but this time Josh and Jacob were persistent. Jimmy slowed down long enough to turn and yell "Suckers!" he called. He hadn't noticed the agile stride of Mrs. Peterson as she walked along the outside wall of the school. He turned to resume running, and she was there.

"Hi, Jimmy." She took his hand.

Josh and Jacob continued to run toward them, and Mrs. Peterson continued to hold Jimmy's hand. These boys weren't exactly angels, either.

"He pushed me in the mud," said Josh in a voice filled with indignation. "We weren't even playing with him."

"I know," said Mrs. Peterson.

"I yelled at him, and Jimmy spit in my face," said Jacob. There were tears in his eyes.

"I know," said Mrs. Peterson. "I saw." She held Jimmy's hand. She looked at the other boys.

"Today, I'm going to handle this problem. Can you get over your anger and play outside today?"

They looked at her and nodded, then started to walk toward the play tower.

"I didn't," muttered Jimmy.

Didn't what? wondered Mrs. Peterson, but she held her tongue. Holding Jimmy's hand, she headed back to her classroom.

After twenty-two years of teaching and the experience of raising four sons of her own, Mrs. Peterson still loved every day in the classroom. She had taught every grade from K to 5, but second grade was her love. The sparkling eyes, emerging skills, and emerging awareness of the seven- and eight-year-olds filled her with fascination and awe. Serving these children gave her the deepest sense of satisfaction, but this year she was worried.

"I didn't do anything," grumbled Jimmy aloud as they walked.

She didn't comment or argue. Jimmy walked willingly with her.

In the month she had known Jimmy in class, she had become more concerned. It wasn't his restlessness. She'd known many fidgety boys. It wasn't the way he sometimes fell out of his chair, or the difficulty he had holding a pencil, or his poor reading skills. He used language pretty well, even if he sometimes misunderstood second grade humor. Somehow she knew he was smart enough.

It was the second day of school when she started to worry, when he looked straight at her and said, "I don't have to do what you say."

They crossed that bridge, and then it was a week later that he walked out of class without asking.

"What are you doing?" she asked him after three quick steps into the hall.

"I'm going to find a bathroom."

"We have our own bathroom," she responded.

"Matthew was just in there," Jimmy replied. "Now it stinks."

It was that look he sometimes had that bothered her. At other times, it was gone, and there were many times when he pushed close to her for warmth or security. Then his look was different.

In the classroom, they hung up their coats and sat down at the back table.

"It was on accident," he told her.

"What was?" Mrs. Peterson asked.

"Pushing him down."

"How about the spitting?" she asked, but he was silent. He glared at the table.

"It's a problem for me when you hurt others," she explained, not for the first time. "Any ideas about how you can solve this problem?"

Already in the first month they'd had this conversation several times. She didn't expect an answer.

"I'm going to call your mom," she explained as she walked to the phone by her desk.

"Right now?" His blue eyes were glistening.

After Mrs. Peterson explained the problem to Jimmy's mother on the phone, there was silence.

"I'm hoping you can come in," said Mrs. Peterson, breaking the silence.

"Do you mean right now?" said Jimmy's mother. "I can't come now. I can't just leave work."

"No, no," said Mrs. Peterson. "Things are fine now. Could you come in after school, or would evening be better?"

They decided on an evening meeting, and at 7:00 P.M. Mrs. Peterson had coffee and tea ready. A few minutes later, Mrs. Jackson arrived. Through her window, Mrs. Peterson was able to watch her as she walked up to the school. It was still light outside. As Mrs. Jackson walked from her car, she stopped and sat on one of the benches outside the front entrance. It seemed as if she was collecting herself, and then for a moment she buried her head in her hands. It was only a moment. She steadied herself and wiped her eyes.

As Mrs. Jackson entered the second grade classroom, Mrs. Peterson thought how young she looked, but tired. Jimmy's mother was nicely dressed, and for a moment they talked about her work and about the fact that Jimmy was her only child.

"I'm worried about some of his behaviors at school," said Mrs. Peterson. "Could you tell me how the school year is going from your perspective at home?"

The dark-haired younger woman looked worried. "Are you getting ready to start kicking him out every day? Please tell me the truth. Is that going to happen again? Last year I almost lost my job."

Mrs. Peterson took a deep breath and looked with care at this younger woman. Lovely, young, tired, worried about Jimmy, concerned that others might think she's an inadequate mother, and strong, Mrs. Peterson noted. There was a strength of character and a commitment to one little boy that she saw in Mrs. Jackson's face.

"No," she responded. "I haven't considered that as yet. And I sincerely hope we never do. I'm hoping we can work together this year and help Jimmy have a much better experience."

"He likes you so far. He really does," said Mrs. Jackson.

"Thank you. I'm very fond of him."

Mrs. Jackson observed her back. "Truly?" she asked.

"Oh, yes."

"My neighbor says I should fight for a Section 504 plan so I could make it much harder for the school to suspend him."

"Really? Do you think that might help?"

"Well, she's had two boys who had an awful time in school and says a mother just has to fight for anything."

"That's so sad," said Mrs. Peterson. For a moment there was silence.

"Do you think I should?" asked Mrs. Jackson sincerely.

"Maybe someday. I can't rule that out for you. But I'm hoping we can find some other options right now."

"I heard you were really good with boys. I asked to have Jimmy put into your class. Did you know that?"

Mrs. Peterson nodded.

"I'll bet you wish I hadn't."

Slowly Mrs. Peterson pulled her chair closer to the young woman. She wanted no table between them. "Did you think I wanted you here tonight to tell you what a bad kid Jimmy is?"

Mrs. Jackson nodded slightly, but did not speak. Mrs. Peterson went on. "Would you like to work with me?"

"What do you mean?"

"Shall we work together this year for as long as it takes to help Jimmy get his behavior and his attention working better? It'll be a lot of work."

"You'd teach me what to do at home?"

Mrs. Peterson smiled. "Everything I can. And if we need help, we'll find it. We can meet here every Monday night, just like this, and we'll develop a plan for home and school."

"You'd do that for me?"

"And for Jimmy," the teacher responded.

A little of the tiredness faded from the young woman's face as they talked that night. The night janitor walked by the room a couple of times and smiled. He'd heard about Jimmy and knew of the other parents Mrs. Peterson had helped in the past.

The first thing they planned to work on at home was getting Jimmy to go to recovery time without a fight. Mrs. Peterson gave Jimmy's mother an audiotape to study.

"Don't try to change much this week," cautioned Mrs. Peterson. "Let's go slowly and get it right."

The following Monday, the two dark-haired women met again. They shared coffee and smiles and concerns.

"Twice I had to carry him to his room for recovery time," recalled Mrs. Jackson. "Then yesterday when I told him we needed a little recovery time, he went all by himself."

"For how long?"

"He was quiet and thinking, so I went to the door after four minutes and told him to feel free to come out whenever he was feeling sweet."

"Did he come out right away?"

"No," Julie Jackson laughed. "I think he wanted to hold on to a little control over when he came out. But a few minutes later he came out and snuggled next to me on the couch."

"I'll bet that felt good," said Mrs. Peterson.

"Yes. He seemed calm." Mrs. Jackson paused. "I really haven't been an adult authority figure for him, have I?"

"No, but that's what you're learning. And you're off to a good start."

Mrs. Jackson smiled at her older friend. "I was hoping that one tape you gave me had everything I needed to know," she said with a twinkle.

"Probably not," said Mrs. Peterson. "But if you want me to, I'll hang in there with you."

Julie Jackson reflected for a moment on her own parenting models and on the choices that led her to the life she knew today. Mrs. Peterson was different. She wasn't big or strong. She wasn't flashy or pushy. There was a quiet resolve about her that Julie knew she needed for her son.

"What's next, Mrs. Peterson? I'm ready."

Mrs. Jackson spent the next few weeks learning to establish herself as the authority figure in the home, but without anger and threats. Once she knew Jimmy would go to recovery time when asked, she practiced getting control over food issues in the house. She cleaned up their diet, made mealtimes much more pleasant, and learned how to handle his whining for sweets.

The little things she practiced made such a difference.

"Jimmy, would you like peas or corn for a vegetable tonight?" she asked, giving him a little control in the right places.

• • • • •

"Would you like a bath or a shower tonight?"

"You know I don't like showers."

"Would you like me to read a story to you while you're taking your bath?"

"Yes, please," said Jimmy.

• • • • •

Sometimes he still screamed at her, and then she practiced some other new skills.

"I will not pick up my clothes. It's your job."

"Oh, Jimmy. It makes me sad when you scream, and I'm not exactly sure what to do about it. But don't worry, I'll get some ideas from my friends. We'll work it out."

Later she might say, "I'll be washing clothes that are put away in the hamper."

·····

On Monday evenings, Mrs. Peterson kept emphasizing empathy.

"But I just want to yell and rip his face off," said Julie Jackson.

"I know the feeling," said Mrs. Peterson. "And how do you think that would work?"

"Not so good. When I use anger and threats, he just resists harder."

"Still, it's hard not to use anger, threats, and lecture," empathized Mrs. Peterson.

Chores weighed heavily on Julie Jackson's mind the night Mrs. Peterson introduced the idea to her.

"He's too young to be responsible for chores," she said aloud. I'll never get him to pay attention to chores, she thought silently. It's easier just to do the work myself.

"Some parents think it's just not worth the effort to get kids to do chores," said Mrs. Peterson. "But if you want Jimmy to keep making progress, it's got to be done."

Somehow, it wasn't as hard as she thought. Jimmy was starting to see his mom as being in charge around the house. He was going to recovery time if asked. He ate what was permitted. Bedtime wasn't an issue.

Jimmy chose taking out the garbage and sweeping the garage as his household jobs. Of course, he had to take care of his own toys and clothes and clear the dishes after meals.

The night Jimmy forgot to push the big garbage container down to the street wasn't really his fault, Julie thought. They'd been out to the school concert, and it was late and Jimmy was tired. She hadn't reminded him.

He was sleeping so soundly as she looked lovingly at him curled up in bed. She started to leave the room and take the garbage out herself, but something stopped her. Gently she shook him.

"Jimmy. It's garbage night."

He opened his eyes and grabbed her hand. "Oh, Mom. I'm tired."

She watched as he put a jacket over his pajamas and his boots over his bare feet and pushed the big container to the street, and somehow she recognized the pride he had in himself for handling his job.

"It was so hard for me," she explained to Mrs. Peterson. "There's a part of me that just wants to protect him from any responsibility. I know it's not respectful of Jimmy, but I still feel it."

After some talk, Mrs. Peterson gave her Dr. Nolan's phone number. She'd worked with him before, and he had a way of helping parents get past the issues related to letting children become more independent. Sometimes parents unconsciously want to keep kids dependent so they'll feel needed by their children. Dr. Nolan dealt with such issues in just a few sessions, and Mrs. Peterson offered to use a special school fund to pay half the fee.

That same night they tackled the topic of TV and video games. By now, there was trust and affection between the two women, and they knew they enjoyed a strong respect for one another. But Julie Jackson looked anxious as Mrs. Peterson described how over-viewing affects young minds. TV was a companion for her.

"Five hours total per week?" she asked the schoolteacher for the second time.

"Of course, it's up to you, but that's what I'd recommend," replied Mrs. Peterson.

"What would we do without the TV on?"

"I've been waiting anxiously to get to that question," said Mrs. Peterson. "Jimmy's behavior is getting so good at school, and now we're ready to help him develop the skills to make learning easy. Can I show you?"

This was the fun part for Mrs. Peterson. She showed Mrs. Jackson how Jimmy's difficulty with balance affected his seatwork and visual-motor skills. She shared the tricks of twenty-two years of teaching and learning. It was hard not to give her young friend too much all at once.

Less TV, lots of coloring, drawing, cutting, Legos, and balance activities on the balance board every day, she described.

It was December. There was a light dusting of snow on the ground. By seven o'clock it was dark, and the two women continued to meet on Mondays. On their last meeting before Christmas vacation, they exchanged small gifts.

In January, Mrs. Peterson looked forward to their first meeting of the new year. Mrs. Jackson and Jimmy had traveled to Buffalo to visit with family. Julie was anxious about the trip. She felt judged by her parents and sister. Jimmy had embarrassed her with his behavior in the past, and on their last visit there had been angry words.

On this Monday night, there were Cub Scouts filtering into the building for den meetings. There was basketball practice in the gymnasium. Mrs. Jackson dusted the snow off her hair as she entered the building and spoke briefly with the school custodian.

Mrs. Peterson was waiting, as usual with coffee. They chatted about holiday things for a moment, then Julie Jackson started to cry, softly at first, then harder. In the quiet of the classroom, Mrs. Peterson wrapped her arms around Julie and held on tight.

After a few moments, Julie told her about their visit, and how scared she had been that she'd be judged harshly again. For the first time since Jimmy was an infant, the visit had gone well. Jimmy and his grandpa had even gone ice-skating together, and once when Jimmy was getting a little wild playing with new toys, Julie had to ask him to go to recovery time for a few minutes and to come back when he was calmer.

"I'll be back in a few minutes, Grandpa," he said as he was leaving. "It won't take me long."

"There was a little incident on the playground today," said Mrs. Peterson. "Want to hear about it?"

"A problem?"

"No. Jimmy was playing with Josh and Jacob, as usual. And I was outside watching the children. I saw the boys running across the field, and Josh tripped and fell, and then came up yelling."

Mrs. Peterson went on. "He was just mad and embarrassed, so he was yelling at Jimmy and accusing Jimmy of tripping him when I walked up."

"Do you need a little help here?" I asked them. "Jimmy just smiled and laughed. 'He's just mad,' Jimmy said. 'Don't worry, we can handle it ourselves.'"

Mrs. Peterson drove home that night through the lightly falling snow. She knew Jimmy and his mom were going to be all right. There was still some vision training to be done, and a few study skills to establish, and some careful reading practice to continue. But she knew.

Her husband met her at the door, and for a few minutes they talked before she excused herself. There was a letter she needed to write tonight.

She settled at her desk and thought about her oldest boy. He was somewhere in East Africa, part of a UNESCO medical team, and she missed him so. He had managed to get a brief call through to her at Christmas, but it was so short. She began to write.

My Dear Jimmy,

I've met another little boy at school this year, and I've been wanting to tell you all about him. His name is also Jimmy. He's going to be fine, partly because of his strong mother, and partly because of all the things you helped me learn when you were his age…

chapter sixteen

Getting Started

Maybe you've smiled and maybe you've cried while reading these chapters. Now you are nearing the end of our book and approaching the opportunity to put together your own plan. We'd like to share a few thoughts on getting started.

Keep It Simple

"I want my child to act responsibly at all times, pick up his clothes, do all his homework without reminders, quit arguing with his sister, quit fighting at school, and treat his parents with respect. That's all."

Reasonable expectations over time, perhaps, but not all this week. For the success of your plan, we advise you to keep it simple. Pick one target behavior at a time. Make a plan. Get the advice or help you need. Then work on that one goal until it is achieved. Give it as long as it takes to become automatic, then move on to your next behavior goal.

Pick Achievable Behavior Goals

Perfectly completed homework without reminders usually can't be expected of a child who is still resisting recovery time and chores. Pick a goal that is achievable. Pick behaviors you are pretty darned sure you can control and begin with a series of successes.

Aim High, Start Slow

- Homework without reminders
- Child is expected to complete assignments at school.
- Child sits in classroom without disturbing others.
- Eliminate defiance in calm, positive ways.
- Chores
- Establish bedtime routine.
- Establish morning routine.
- Resolve food control issues.
- Recovery time
- Set limits by using Thinking Words.
- Neutralize arguments.

Rehearse

If Love and Logic is new to you, implement it a little at a time. Pick one thing about your child's behavior that you think you have a good opportunity to change and then work on it. But don't begin right away. Take time to rehearse your first efforts. Practice using enforceable statements or neutralizing arguments. Figure out your child's possible responses. Talk it over with your spouse or friend. Picture yourself trying out your new techniques. Practice until something inside of you says, "I'm ready. Come on, kid. Make my day!"

Be Patient

Be patient with yourself, because it's hard to change. At times, you'll think you're ready to use Love and Logic, and somehow words of anger or hovering will come out. No problem. Your kids will survive.

Talk to your friends that use Love and Logic. Reread portions of this book or listen to Love and Logic tapes to help you review the ideas you've decided to try. The research on spaced repetition tells us we have a better chance of using a new idea if we revisit it six to eight times. Listening, rereading, talking, or teaching helps us learn to use techniques that are different than the models we hold from childhood.

Be patient with your children as well. It takes about one month of
Love and Logic parenting to undo one year of ineffective parenting.
Your child may expect that this is just another phase and predict that
you will go back to your old ways. Some kids may try to blow your new
techniques out of the water by pushing your anger, sympathy, or guilt
buttons. Just hang in there. With every success you experience, your
self-concept will develop. With each of your successes, your children
will see you demonstrating self-respect as well as respect toward them.
It's never too late to begin to use Love and Logic.

Network

There is strength in collaboration. In times past, neighbors kept a close
eye on all the local children and didn't hesitate to walk little Foster
home if he was misbehaving. Extended families lived close together and
shared responsibilities, including the rearing of children.

Many parents today do not have strong networks of support. Families
are spread out across the country. Neighbors may not even know each
other. We're afraid to discipline other people's children.

It's ironic. In the last twenty years, we've shared the teachings of Love
and Logic with hundreds of thousands of people. There are more great
resources, including books, videos, and audiotapes on parenting than ever
before. And yet more parents today are isolated, struggling to parent without the benefit of good information or good support for their efforts.

Some churches are stepping forward to prioritize helping families. As
you know from reading this book, we believe that schools can do a lot
more to help, and many have begun. Occasionally there are neighborhood
support systems and families that reach out to help a member who is
struggling to raise strong children.

It is our hope and prayer that the ideas in this book will be shared.
Every family needs to lean on others for help from time to time.
Sharing with others and learning from others is part of learning to
raise wonderful kids.

Some neighbors gather once a month just to talk about a parenting issue or discuss a book. Some churches offer regular Love and Logic workshops and also offer parent support networks. Some brothers and sisters rotate new books or tapes with their siblings. Some schools have wonderful parent libraries with comfortable chairs and a hot pot of coffee.

There is strength in collaboration. Our kids share ideas, excuses, and tips for handling parents with each other. Effective parents establish strong networks of support so that they can maintain the mental, emotional, spiritual, physical, and energetic resources to be great moms and dads.

Celebrate Each Success

Somehow it's true. Those things we give energy and attention grow within our lives. If we spend all of our time grumbling about how disappointed we are by life, we get more disappointment. If we notice the wonderful traits of our children, they grow. If we practice an attitude of gratitude for all the blessings we have, they increase.

Love and Logic parents get loud and rambunctious about positive behavior. We notice it and enjoy it. We give it energy.

When our children make poor choices, we get empathetic and our voices get soft. We give energy to the thought that they are capable of learning by experience. We take good care of ourselves while we allow natural and logical consequences to do the teaching.

Love and Logic parents get loud about good behavior and soft about poor behavior.

Bring Joy into Your Home

Every week we hear stories and receive letters from parents telling how their lives have changed since they began to practice Love and Logic. Some report that things are a whole lot calmer in their homes and in their lives. Others report that their kids are happier. Sometimes even marriages improve.

But Love and Logic is just one piece in the process of bring joy into your home. Great parents do more.

Talking to parents all around the country gives us ideas and stories and also inspires us to share the wonders of parenting with joy. Parents tell us about their family traditions, including storytelling, listening time, and helping others in need. Great parents are almost always good listeners, and they model respect for others in all aspects of their lives. They model living joyfully and celebrating mistakes and demonstrate an attitude of gratitude for the people and opportunities in their lives. They reach out to others, and at times, they let others reach out to them.

· · · · ·

I was shopping at Target when I saw him. Actually, I heard him first from the next aisle over.

"I want cookies."

"Put them back now. We can't get everything you want."

"I want it."

"Roger, please be good. Now give me the box."

The begging went on, and then for a moment there was silence as I came around the end of the aisle. He was clutching his cookie box with a smirk on his face, assuming victory. Then he spied the Cracker Jacks. He tossed the cookies into the cart and went for the next treat, but his exasperated mother blocked him.

"No, Roger. No more."

"Yes, I want them."

"No more." She grabbed his hand and jerked him hard down the aisle toward me.

"That sucks," he responded loudly.

She turned to Roger. "Don't you use that word. Don't you ever talk that way. I mean it!"

She was right in his face. He paused, then replied, "Suck, suck, suck, suck, suck."

I held my tongue and passed them in the aisle. Later as I was finishing my shopping, I saw them again in the checkout line. Roger was busily chewing on a caramel sucker. I could have pulled into another line, but instead I got behind them and struck up a conversation.

Roger's mother was young, but looked tired. She recognized me from the Cracker Jack aisle and looked embarrassed. Roger was busy with his sucker.

"It's rough raising kids these days," I commented.

Moving closer to me and speaking softly, Roger's mother spoke words that still touch my heart. "I just wanted a little baby. And now sometimes I think I hate him."

We spoke in the checkout lane for a few minutes. When she'd paid for her goods, I offered to give her a tape, just for a few laughs. Getting a copy of the "Life-Saver Kit" from the car, I wished her luck.

Normally, I try not to butt into other people's lives unless they ask for ideas, but something pulled me to offer the tapes, and that's not the end of the story. A couple of months later, she called. Here is what Roger's mother said.

• • • • •

Things are just starting to change around here, she reported. I've been thinking about your tapes, and talking to my mom and my friends. I guess I'm feeling there's some hope for the future.

I particularly like knowing that I don't have to deal with every situation right now, she explained. It's alright for me to say, "This is so sad. I'm going to have to do something. But not here. I don't want to embarrass you."

I like remembering to whisper and grin when I want to be heard. And the empathy, that's hard for me at times, but I'm practicing.

Shopping with Roger has always been a problem. I listened to the tapes, and talked about my plan with my mother. It's a good thing, too. She reminded me that sometimes he drops to the ground and kicks and won't get up. My friend offered to shadow me in the store in case Roger decided to drop.

Then I was ready. I went shopping and I expected the usual. He started begging for stuff, then he grabbed a toy.

"Oh, Roger," I smiled. "Do you think that might be a bad decision? Try not to worry, but I'm going to have to do something about it."

He was so shocked that he gave up the toy, and we left the store and went straight home.

The next morning, I got ready for shopping.

"Guess what," I told Roger. "Today I get to go shopping without arguments, and without anyone saying 'suck, suck, suck'. And Roger, you're going to have your first opportunity to hire your own babysitter."

My friend Doris had offered to be my Mabel. I had the greatest time shopping. I even remembered to be just finishing my hot fudge sundae as I came home.

"I'm glad to see you," I honestly told him when I got home.

His eyes were so big when he had to pay for the babysitter with his Galactic Space Raider. I almost went weak at that point because he looked so sad. But I'm glad I didn't. He wanted to pay Mabel with some of his old, unwanted toys. But I knew he needed to make a real sacrifice in order for the training to be of value.

Two days later we were at McDonalds. I didn't have a lot of money. I just had enough for a Happy Meal for him and a hamburger and coffee for me. He wanted an apple pie, but I didn't have enough. I was afraid he might throw another fit, but instead he just turned quietly away from me. I could hear him saying softly to himself, "This sucks."

Things aren't perfect. And I still have a lot to practice, but Roger and I are going to make it.

······❤······

Adaptation Plan

Student: _____ B.D.: _____ Age: _____ Date:
Parent(s)/Guardian(s): _____ Phone: _____

STATEMENT OF CONCERN
_____

STUDENT'S STRENGTHS
_____

STUDENT'S WEAKNESSES
_____

ADAPTATIONS NEEDED
_____

ADDITIONAL LEARNING TASKS
_____

| _____ | _____ | _____ |
| Teacher Signature | Student Signature | Parent Signature |

RECOMMENDED SERVICES OR ADAPTATIONS

1. Insist that student keeps assignment sheet or notebook. Check to ensure that they are accurate and up to date.
2. Present all class assignments in oral and written form.
3. Modify assignments as necessary.
4. Modify class objectives and grading system.
5. Reduce the length of written assignments.
6. Provide alternatives to written assignments for a student with written language difficulty.
7. Sign the student's assignment book on a daily/weekly basis.
8. Provide extended test time.
9. Allow students to use special education test taking support services, if eligible.
10. Provide alternative forms of assessment, as appropriate.
11. Teach how to plan work for assigned tests.
12. When possible, allow students to record answers on the test rather than an answer sheet.
13. Make sure student's work area is clear of unnecessary materials that might serve as distractions.
14. Use graph paper to help students organize math papers.
15. Permit students with poor penmanship to respond verbally and present papers orally.
16. For older students with poor penmanship, encourage the use of a typewriter or word processor.
17. Provide ample "wait time" for student who may have difficulty answering questions.
18. Periodically, review student's notes to ensure that the most important information is being recorded.
19. Summarize key points of a lesson to make sure important information has been recorded.
20. Allow a peer with good note-taking skills to use NCR paper when copying notes. The copy can be given to the student with less developed skills.

21. Try a "study buddy" for the distractible student.
22. Provide large print materials.
23. Use a study carrel within the classroom.
24. Send progress reports home every week.
25. Allow use of a tape recorder during lecture.
26. Encourage the use of a calculator.
27. Allow the student opportunities to move in the classroom, as appropriate.
28. Assign seating near the front of the classroom.
29. _____

_____

_____

_____

_____

30. _____

_____

_____

_____

_____

RECOMMENDED ADDITIONAL STUDENT LEARNING TASKS

1. Set timelines for major projects.
2. Review your understanding of a written assignment with your teacher on a regular basis.
3. Practice appropriate requests for support.
4. Develop note-taking skills.
5. Develop outlining skills.
6. Learn to make a mind-map.
7. Keep a daily assignment log.
8. Form a study group.
9. Keep a list of required materials for each class.
10. _____

_____

_____

_____

_____

11. _____

_____

_____

_____

_____

ANY PUBLIC SCHOOL
Adaptation Plan

Student: William H.   B.D.: 11/21/84   Age: 15   Date: 1/30/00
Parent(s)/Guardian(s): Roy/Betty   Phone: 344-8443

STATEMENT OF CONCERN
Bill needs extra time to perform written tasks because of slow hand-writing speed and difficulty with organization. Please also observe for periods of distractibility and share observations with Mrs. Janer.

STUDENT'S STRENGTHS
Good listening and verbal skills, ability to notice visual detail and artistic ability.

STUDENT'S WEAKNESSES
Visual-motor development, handwriting, distractibility at times.

ADAPTATIONS NEEDED
Reduce written assignments, particularly evening assignments when medication has worn off; use an NCR notetaker when apropriate; check assignment book weekly; and use special education test support services (see back).

ADDITIONAL LEARNING TASKS
Maintain a regular, daily schedule at home, show daily assignment log to parents each day, practice appropriate requests for support at school and review one school success with parents each week.

_____   _____   _____
  Teacher Signature   Student Signature   Parent Signature

How I Learn Best

How I Learn Best

INTRODUCTION

No two human beings think, perceive, process and organize information from the world around us in precisely the same way. We are unique, and one of the challenges of your uniqueness is to discover how to learn, relate, and succeed in a way that's best suited to you.

"How I Learn Best" is designed to help you recognize how you think, learn, organize, and perceive, so that you can use this information to help you succeed.

Lifelong learning is no longer just an option. Futurists and employers alike tell us that young people today will hold several jobs with significantly different skill requirements. No longer can you develop one skill and expect to be successful or employable for a lifetime. We need now to become a nation of learners.

The contents of this booklet are only a beginning. It is my hope that you will talk with your friends, parents, or teachers and get their insight on how to apply what you learn. Or you may choose to do some more reading on these topics, or write down your thoughts, or choose any process that suits you to help you become a successful lifelong learner. Best of luck!

TYPES OF INTELLIGENCE

There are many ways of thinking and learning. Identify which of the following uses of intelligence best describes you:

Circle the number that fits you best.
5 = Yes, that's me   3 = Sort of   1 = Not like me

1. **Verbal/Linguistic:** I like reading and under-   5   4   3   2   1
    standing what I read and communicating
    through writing and speaking.

2. **Logical/Mathematical:** I like doing math in   5   4   3   2   1
    my head, thinking logically, problem solving,
    and I'm good at making change with money.

3. **Spatial:** I enjoy drawing, painting, or working   5   4   3   2   1
    with clay. I can find my way by using a map
    and I can create interesting pictures in my mind.

4. **Body/Kinesthetic:** I like movement, including   5   4   3   2   1
    exercising, physical sports, or dance. I like
    action and feel that I use my body with skill.

5. **Musical/Rhythmic:** I can remember musical   5   4   3   2   1
    tunes and recognize the sound of different
    instruments from a recording. I enjoy singing
    or playing music.

6. **Interpersonal:** I am a good listener, supportive   5   4   3   2   1
    of others, and do my part when I'm a member
    of a group or team. I like to work with others.

7. **Intrapersonal:** I know myself fairly well. I'm   5   4   3   2   1
    thoughtful and aware of my personal beliefs
    and feelings. I like to do some things alone.

SENSORY PREFERENCE

By identifying your learning strengths and preferences, you can begin to identify strategies that will help you learn in the best way for you. Identifying your sensory learning preference is another important piece of information. We primarily identify visual (seeing), auditory (hearing), tactile (touch), and kinesthetic (movement) preferences for learning. Humans use all four modes and certainly need to develop our skills in each area. But we each have preferences for how we prefer to integrate experience or knowledge into our consciousness. Which sensory preferences are yours?

Circle the number that fits you best.
5 = Strong Preference   3 = Moderate Preference   1 = Low Preference

1. **Visual:** I remember what I see, like phone numbers or spelling words or words in a book. Sometimes I draw or doodle or make visual models of how ideas fit together. I've noticed that I use phrases like, "I see what you mean," or "That looks right to me." How things appear is important to me, and some people say I'm a fast talker. I gather information well by reading.

   5   4   3   2   1

2. **Auditory:** I listen well. Sometimes I'm surprised others do not hear conversations as accurately as I do. I like the sound of a good voice or a good piece of music. I remember a phone number or a math fact or poetry by hearing it a few times. I don't need to take a lot of notes in class. I can comprehend and condense the main ideas and then write them down. I've noticed that I sometimes say "I hear you," or "That sounds right to me."

   5   4   3   2   1

3. **Kinesthetic:** I love to learn by experiences,   5 4 3 2 1
   like going on a trip, building something, per-
   forming experiments, or working on a project. I get tired of sitting still for long periods.
   I like to move. I'm good at rhythmical movement and can recall games, dances, sports,
   and/or directions after I've physically performed them a few times. Sometimes I say
   things like, "This is how I feel about it," or "It
   just feels right."

PERCEPTION AND ORGANIZATION

Each human being perceives and organizes information from the world around us in a unique
way. Dr. Anthony Gregorc and Dr. Bernice
McCarthy have developed processes to help us
identify where we fit among the four dominant
styles identified in their research. See which style
best describes you.

Circle the number that fits you best.
5 = Yes, that's me   3 = Sort of 1 = Not like me

1. **Concrete Sequential:** I'm a practical, persist-   5 4 3 2 1
   ent, stable person. I like to accomplish tasks
   using a careful sequence of steps. I like to see
   that my world is in order. Perhaps I'm not the
   most creative person, but I get things done. I
   take direction well. I don't take unnecessary
   risks, and I'm realistic.

2. **Abstract Sequential:** I am an analytic thinker.   5 4 3 2 1
   I use logical thought to understand my world.
   I work carefully and have high standards for

myself. I like to learn in an orderly environment
where I get to analyze ideas and concepts.
I use language precisely, and I don't jump
to conclusions.

3. **Abstract Random:** I am sensitive, colorful,   5   4   3   2   1
   lively and spontaneous. I'm a good listener
   and am aware of the needs of others. I am
   intuitive and artistic and not always on time.
   I'll never be an accountant, but I try to bring
   out the best in people.

4. **Concrete Random:** I like to think for myself,   5   4   3   2   1
   get things done, and I don't mind a little
   competition. I like choices and do not enjoy
   being told there is only one way to accomplish
   a task. Give me the freedom to use my own
   ideas, and I'll get the job done well. I'm intuitive and energetic and see possibilities that
   others sometimes overlook.

WHAT WORKS FOR ME

It's important for me to be aware of what practices help me study or
learn most effectively. The following is a summary of what works best
for me:

*When I try to learn by **listening** to a lecture, discussion, or tape:*
   I read about the subject beforehand.
   I take careful notes.
   I ask questions, if appropriate.
   I draw a visual model to represent the main ideas.
   I record and listen again in a relaxing atmosphere.
   I write the main ideas and then write out my thoughts in detail at
   a later time.

I gather with others to discuss the concepts later.

I try to use the information in some practical way so that I can better understand its application.

I always check with the instructor to verify that I understand the main ideas.

I get someone who is a great note-taker to share notes so I can listen with greater attention.

Other _____

_____

_____

_____

Other _____

_____

_____

_____

When I am trying to learn from **reading:**

I write out notes as I go.

I read first for concept, then later for detail.

I usually go to a quiet place.

I usually read with a study buddy to keep me on task.

I usually read with music to help me focus.

I draw visual models to create a mental picture of important contents or details.

I record the main ideas on a tape as I read.

I use a study group to discuss the reading.

I try to share the main ideas I have read with my study buddy.

I use a highlighter.

I write notes in the margin of the books.

I close my eyes, rest the book on my head, and hope it sinks in.

Other _____

_____

_____

Other _____

_____

_____

_____

When I am trying to learn from **group work:**

I take detailed notes as we work.

I record audio notes on a tape as we work.

I write down only the major points as we work then write out my thoughts in detail after the group work.

I check for understanding with my study buddy.

I draw a visual model of any concepts discussed or plans made.

Other _____

_____

_____

Other _____

_____

_____

When I am trying to **learn by doing,** *as in a lab, or on the job:*

I ask lots of questions.

I observe someone who seems to have skill at this activity.

I keep a log of activities and reflections.

I summarize an activity or a busy day with a written or audiotaped reflection.

I seek out someone each day to discuss what we learned.

I practice any new and challenging skill at home.

I practice actually using my new skill or procedure several times on my own.

I practice by visualizing the steps of an activity.

I draw a visual model of new skills or procedures.

I try to teach the ideas or information to someone else to be sure I understand and can articulate my understanding.

Other _____

_____

_____

Other _____

_____

_____

*When I am trying to **stay alert and on-task** even if I am doing something boring:*

I work for short periods and take breaks.

I listen to attention-enhancing music.

I isolate myself from distractions.

I exercise before trying to concentrate.

I keep healthy food nearby.

I reward myself when I've reached my goal.

I work with a study buddy.

I work on difficult tasks at a time of day that works best for me.

I set specific daily goals for what I want to accomplish.

Other _____

_____

_____

Other _____

_____

_____

DAILY HABITS

These are the habits that help me to stay organized and self-disciplined (check the habits you practice every working day):

I exercise in the morning.

I take time for a good breakfast.

I write a daily plan.

I reserve a period of quiet time for myself each morning.

I keep my work for the day in a special place.

I talk with a friend about the day to come.

I arrive early to my daily appointments.

I use a tape recorder to keep daily notes.

I use a note-taker, as needed.

I participate in a regular study group.

I ask for oral reading of tests, as needed.

I request additional time for tests, as needed.

I keep notes in a laptop computer.

I check with instructors after each class to be sure I understand the assignments.

I take regular exercise/movement breaks throughout the day.

I exercise each afternoon.

I maintain a regular time for study.

I spend ten minutes or more developing an important skill each day.

I take time each day to enjoy something I do well.

I maintain a healthy diet.

I exercise in the evening.

I do something for someone else each day.

I keep a journal.

I review my goals for the next day.

I maintain positive relationships.

I maintain a place of study that works well for me.

I choose to read/study in a place with dim/moderate/bright light.

I work on difficult assignments at a time of day when I am at my best.

Other _____

_____

_____

Other _____

_____

_____

_____

Summary Statement

I stay organized and self-disciplined when I _____

_____

_____

_____

_____

_____

MY TEACHING STYLE PREFERENCE

When I have a choice, I look for teachers/mentors with the following characteristics. When I need to learn something and do not have a choice, I adjust my daily habits so I can learn well from any good instructor.

Select the ten characteristics you most prefer in a teacher:

Clearly stated and sequenced learning objectives for the class.

An easygoing approach to what materials we may cover.

A clear statement of the main objectives of the class and the flexibility to meet these objectives in multiple ways.

Makes study guides available.

Use of lecture.

Use of personal storytelling.

Use of videos.

Emphasis on group work.

Many projects.

Use of essay tests.

Use of multiple choice tests.

Allows demonstration of skills learned through projects.

Uses colorful language.

Talks fast/slowly.

Uses overheads.

Engages the class in discussion.

Challenges our ideas.

Logical and analytic.

Begins class on time.

Acknowledges the work of experts in the field.

Allows students to express their own ideas.

Has time after class for students.

Use of an objective grading system.

Makes everyone feel supported.

Enjoys competition.

Isn't afraid to acknowledge mistakes.

Keeps the class on task.

Helps me see how each bit of information fits together into a pattern.

Emphasizes learning from experience.

Demonstrates a good sense of history.

Clearly tells me what to do and when it is due.

Encourages creativity.

Tells jokes.

Moves quickly through the material.

Assigns a lot of reading out of class.

Emphasizes writing.

Plays music while teaching.

Gives few time limits to complete work.

Encourages participation in class discussion.

Allows us to take work home.

Summarizes the learning objective at the beginning and end of a class.
Hands out a syllabus for the entire course.
Allows students to eat/drink in class.
Frequently checks for understanding when teaching.
Gives personal attention to each student.
Frequently writes on the chalkboard.
Frequently checks for student progress through quizzes.
Asks questions to see if students understand the material.
Emphasizes small group work.
Uses a text as the primary source of information.
Assigns reading from many different sources.

Summarize the teaching style you prefer.

_____
_____
_____
_____
_____

LEARNING SKILLS I WOULD LIKE TO DEVELOP

After identifying my learning preferences and strengths, it is also clear to me that I would like to improve some of my learning skills. For each skill, I will attach a brief plan of improvement. For example:

Desired Skill: Learn to be a better listener

Plan of Improvement:
1. I will take the listening training course available at the community college.
2. I will practice listening before speaking in any groups.
3. I will take five minutes to clear my mind of busy thoughts when I feel anxious.

Desired Skill:_____

Plan of Improvement: _____

_____

_____

_____

_____

Desired Skill:_____

Plan of Improvement: _____

_____

_____

_____

_____

Desired Skill:_____

Plan of Improvement: _____

_____

_____

_____

_____

Desired Skill:_____

Plan of Improvement: _____

_____

_____

_____

_____

Index